Pse return to

Jim Forwood

A History of
ST. PAUL'S CHURCH, SKETTY, SWANSEA

F. G. COWLEY

*With a chapter on the stained glass
and decorative art
by Professor Maurice Broady*

Published by
Vicar and Churchwardens
St. Paul's Church, Sketty, Swansea

Published in 2001 by
Vicar and Churchwardens
St. Paul's Church
Sketty, Swansea

ISBN 0-9539962-0-4

Printed and bound in Wales by
Dinefwr Press Ltd.
Rawlings Road, Llandybie
Carmarthenshire, SA18 3YD

Front cover:
Mosaics by Antonio Salviati
(*J. Beynon*)

Back cover:
Lectern drop
(*J. Beynon*)

This book is dedicated
to the memory of
my beloved wife Jane

Contents

Page

List of Illustrations

COLOUR ILLUSTRATIONS

Foreword

In May 2000, when I arrived as Vicar of Sketty, I was very pleased to find that arrangements for celebrating the 150th Anniversary of the Consecration of the Church and of the Founding of the Parish were well in hand. I was particularly pleased to learn that a history of St Paul's Church and Parish, a permanent commemoration of what we were and where we are, was being prepared.

My own memories go back to the front row of the choir in the late 1950s, perhaps a rather restricted viewpoint. Dr Cowley's survey of the whole span of Parish life down the years is very different. It is also of the first importance, for when we know where we come from it is easier to set our goals for a Parish that, after a century and a half, is still very much a going concern! A new millennium, a changing society, possibilities beyond our forebears' dreams: this is the context in which we take responsibility for continuing the best of what has gone before, and making our own witness to a Christian faith that is both old and ever new.

I speak for the Parish in expressing our gratitude to Dr Cowley and all who have assisted him. I believe that all who read this account will find it not only informative, but also an inspiration to engage with a new phase in the life of a magnificent Church.

CANON ANDREW J. KNIGHT
November 2000

Preface

When, some years ago, the then vicar, Canon Robert Williams (now Archdeacon of Gower), invited me to write the history of St. Paul's, Sketty, I at first declined. I was, after all, a member of another parish who rarely visited St. Paul's except to attend weddings and funerals. I had, too, not long before, written historical accounts of a number of Gower churches and was suffering from a mild bout of what might be called 'ecclesiological fatigue'. Then, however, I recalled that I had a few years earlier delivered a paper to the Welsh Ecclesiastical History Society on the history of St. Paul's during the Victorian period. I soon persuaded myself that with the late Harry Williams' centenary history at my elbow, I would be able to complete the work with a minimum of effort and in record time. But once I had started to sift through the records of St. Paul's in the West Glamorgan Archive Service, I realised how misplaced my optimism had been. St. Paul's is such a high profile church that it deserved something more than a hastily-written hack job.

One major stumbling block which confronted me from the start was the loss of the file of parish magazines before 1959. These would have provided easily accessible material on the history of the fabric and on the stained glass. My friend Dr. Geoffrey Orrin came to my aid here and drew my attention to the records of the Incorporated Church Building Society, now housed at Lambeth Palace Library, which had files on the major extensions made to the church in 1907 and 1928-9. Dr. Orrin also furnished me with the reference to the rare, early photograph of the Revd. M.E. Welby. I was relieved of the difficult task of researching and writing on the stained glass and decorative art by the kindness of Professor Maurice Broady. An acknowledged authority on the stained glass of our area, he readily agreed to write the important chapter on these subjects. I am deeply grateful to him. I also owe a special debt of gratitude to my friend Professor John Beynon who patiently and expertly took general views of the exterior and interior of the church and more detailed photographs of the furnishings and stained glass. The portfolio of slides and prints he supplied saved me from doubling the number of journeys I had to make to the church and has also furnished me with a number of the fine photographs which illustrate the book.

The late vicar, Canon Robert Williams, and his secretary, sacristan and verger, Sue Knight, have been consistently helpful in supplying me with important information on the church and in opening the church and making its treasures available for photographing. The Revd. Roger Brown, a former parishioner, now Vicar of Wrexham, patiently answered a number of my questions and also allowed me to see some of his unpublished articles. I am also grateful to Bishop Anthony, who, when I casually asked him for a suitable title for Chapter 3, immediately responded with the appropriate lines of a hymn. Other clergy who have supplied important pieces of information are the Revd. Martin J. Batchelor, the Revd. Chancellor Arthur Howells, the Revd. Canon E.T. Hunt, the Venerable David Brian James, the late Canon A.L.F. Norman, Canon J. Nigel Rowe (Kilvert Society), the Venerable Ilar Roy Luther Thomas, the Revd. Chancellor David Walker and the Revd. Jennifer Wigley.

Lay people within and outside the parish have also supplied useful information. They include: Miss Linda Chaplin, Mrs. Carol Edwards, Dr. Ian and Mrs. Barbara Graham, the late Mr. Alan Hughes and Mrs. Elaine Hughes, Mrs. Marjorie James, Mrs. Susan James, Mrs. Iris Jones, Mrs. Vivienne Lewis, Mr. Alan Mone, Mrs. Ann Morgan, Mrs. Wendy Phelan, Miss Joyce Phillips, Mr. Bryan and Mrs. Ennis Roberts, Miss Elizabeth Rhodes, Mrs. Hilary Rose, Mrs. F.W. Thomas, Mr. Iorwerth Thomas and Lady Fay Williams.

Research can be never-ending. There is always new material to find and exploit; there are always knowledgeable people yet to interview with important information to impart. Yet there comes a time when one has to call a halt to the pleasurable process of collecting material and to set about the more difficult task of reducing the material collected to an orderly and connected narrative. That point was reached early in 1999. This meant I was not able to benefit from using Christopher Harris and Richard Startup's *The Church in Wales . . .* (Cardiff, 1999) nor D. Densil Morgan's *The Span of the Cross: Christian Religion and Society in Wales, 1914-2000* (Cardiff, 1999). I regret too that I have not yet been able to consult the doctoral theses of Peter Freeman on the Oxford Movement in Wales and of L.A. Cook on the Vivian family.

Miss Susan Beckley and her staff at the West Glamorgan Archive Service, especially Mr. Kim Collis and Mr. Gwyn Davies, have been of enormous help while I worked my way through the St. Paul's archive. They were always ready with good advice and readily arranged for photocopies and photographs to be made of some of the material. The staff of the City and County of Swansea Central Reference Library have been equally helpful over a long period in making available material from their rich local collections and from their invaluable cuttings file. I owe a special debt to

Mrs. Marilyn Jones, the Local Studies Librarian, and supervisor of the Cambrian Newspaper Project. She retrieved for me important pieces of information on a number of topics and especially on the Revd. M.E. Welby and also supplied me with photographs of items in the Library's collections. The Keeper and staff of the Manuscripts Room at the National Library of Wales have been extremely helpful over a long period and have made available to me there valuable material from the Vivian and Church in Wales collections. I have to thank too the staff of the Swansea Museum, especially Bernice Cardy, for many kindnesses and for allowing me access to the files of the *Cambrian* newspaper.

My rather messy handwritten manuscript was expertly typed for me by Mrs. Gloria Watkins of Word for Word, Brynaman. It was then passed to Churchwarden Dr. Jim Davies who cast a careful, experienced, editorial eye over what I had written and saved me from a number of errors of punctuation, grammar and fact and has been fully involved in the publication process. I am deeply indebted to them both.

I have attempted as full an account as possible and have tried hard to be accurate in the facts presented and to be as impartial as I could in my judgements. But I must take full responsibility for the errors which remain. Finally, I would like to wish the Revd. Canon Andrew Knight, the newly-appointed vicar, a long, happy and fruitful ministry at St. Paul's and to thank him for writing the Foreword.

F.G. Cowley
West Cross
November 2000

CHAPTER 1

From Tractarianism to Evangelicalism, 1850-1914

The Background

On 2nd August 1850 the Revd. John Mason Neale, the ecclesiologist and hymn writer, used the newly-opened South Wales Railway to travel down to Swansea. Once settled into the Castle Hotel, Wind St., he wrote to his wife recounting his impressions of the railway and his journey. 'The night entrance into Swansea,' he wrote, 'is awfully beautiful. I can imagine no scene on earth more nearly resembling hell. I have seen the Birmingham and Newcastle works by night, but they are not to be compared for ghastly effect to the green flames of the copper furnaces. Get Mr. Burt to show you the last [London] *Illustrated News*; there you will see the Landore viaduct from the top of which this effect is chiefly gained.' When Neale looked out over the lower Swansea Valley as his train crossed Brunel's creaking wooden viaduct, the Dantesque scene that met his eyes was largely the creation of the Vivian and Sons' Copper Works and was closely connected with the purpose of his visit, for Neale had specially travelled down to Swansea to view and report on the Vivian family's newly-built church at Sketty.

The copper works at Hafod had been started by the Cornishman John Henry Vivian in 1809 and by the middle of the century was beginning to dominate the economy of the lower Swansea Valley and the town. John Henry devoted part of his newly acquired wealth to building the castellated mansion at Singleton Abbey. He surrounded it with an elegant park and began laying the foundations of a modest landed estate. His eldest son, Henry Hussey, after an unhappy spell at Eton, where he was bullied, was sent to France and Germany to obtain a grounding in the technical and commercial aspects of the metals trade and thence to Trinity College, Cambridge. Trinity, with nearly five hundred students, was the largest and perhaps the most prestigious of the Cambridge colleges at this time, and more importantly was an influential centre of Tractarian theology and ritual innovation. John Mason Neale, a contemporary of Henry Hussey at

Trinity, was at the centre of this influence, for in 1839 he founded, with his friend Benjamin Webb the Cambridge Camden Society. Initially this was little more than a student society whose main object was to study church architecture and the furniture of Christian worship by visiting and recording local churches. Gradually, however, through the society's journal *The Ecclesiologist* which began publication in 1841, and through a growing country-wide membership, it became an influential pressure group for propagating what it considered to be correct standards for the building and furnishing of churches. What eventually became the standard canons of taste of the Camden (after 1846 the Ecclesiological) Society may be briefly summarised.

Churches should only be built in the Gothic style of architecture and the Decorated or mid-pointed style of Gothic was to be preferred. The Society preached a crusade against appropriated box pews, galleries and three-decker pulpits which cluttered churches and obscured the congregation's view of the altar. The altar should be given prominence, raised on steps at the east end and the chancel should have stalls for the clergy and choir, separate from the congregation who were to be seated in free, unappropriated seats. The Cambridge Ecclesiologists expressed the aesthetic and architectural ideals of the Oxford or Tractarian movement whose main preoccupation had been theology. Both schools of thought fused to produce an Anglo-Catholic party in the Church of England. J.M. Neale was to achieve fame as a composer of hymns and as a brilliant translator of the Latin and Greek hymns of the early and medieval church and both groups are generously represented in *Hymns Ancient and Modern* and the *English Hymnal.* Among the more memorable are Jerusalem the Golden, O Come O Come Emmanuel, All Glory Laud and Honour, the Royal Banners Forward Go. But when he came to Swansea in 1850 he would have been principally known as an ecclesiologist and high churchman.

Henry Hussey Vivian did not finish his degree course and graduate at Trinity, for with the resignation of J.P. Budd in 1841 the Vivians' Liverpool office became vacant. He took over the Liverpool office in 1842 and in 1845 transferred to Hafod, Swansea, as general manager under his father. His diary during this period shows that his religious views had been deeply influenced by his two years at Trinity College. 'If it is to be one thing or the other let it be Pusey,' he wrote in 1844. 'I have a horror of Puritans but Pusey may carry it too far for weak minds.' Again, in a revealing entry a month later in London: 'Mr. Bennett at St. Paul's on the Communion. Much struck with his sermon. I fear I am anything but what I should be with a decided aversion to religious thought. I have never communicated [he was now twenty-three]. Why not? I am a very light

Henry Hussey Vivian, *c.*1850
(City and County of Swansea: Swansea Museum)

thinker, and during church it is seldom I keep my thoughts fixed. I try hard to do so but can't. I am resolved to think more of religious objects, but the eternal din of business drives all other thoughts out of my head. I certainly feel well with the Pusies. The only thing I objected to today was that he wished all charity to go to the priests.' As a young man, then, Henry Hussey was a Tractarian, a disciple of the Oxford movement, but with niggling reservations about the dangers of the doctrine of the apostolic succession, the belief that the priest derived his powers from Christ by the laying on of hands from apostolic times. It was an ancient doctrine, forcibly restated in 1833 by John Henry Newman in Tract I addressed to Anglican priests:

> We have been born, not of blood, nor of the will of the flesh, nor of the will of man, but of God. The Lord Jesus Christ gave His Spirit to His Apostles; they in turn laid their hands on those who should succeed them; and these again on others; and so the sacred gift has been handed down to our present Bishops, who have appointed us as their assistants, and in some sense representatives . . . it is the doctrine of the Ordination Service . . .

The reservations which Henry Hussey had about this doctrine were to loom larger in his mind as the years passed but as yet were little more than faint flecks of cloud on a distant horizon.

If the foundation of St. Paul's church is to be seen in proper perspective something needs to be said briefly of religion and the Church in Swansea at this time. Sketty and the Vivian estate lay in the parish of St. Mary's, Swansea. St. Mary's was the premier church of the old deanery of Gower which by this time had been divided into the two deaneries of East and West Gower. Originally built in the twelfth century to serve the garrison of the castle and the burgesses of the town, it had been rebuilt in the early fourteenth century, perhaps under the influence and patronage of 'the Wykeham of South Wales', the builder-bishop of St. David's, Henry de Gower (1328-47). Had this Decorated style church survived in its entirety, it would certainly have been a model of ecclesiological rectitude and delighted Neale but in 1737 the roof of the nave caved in. The old nave was taken down and a hideous new nave built. When Sir Stephen Glynne, a noted describer of churches visited it he called the style of the new nave 'ugly – pseudo-Italian' and declared that the 'interior with its pues [sic], galleries and cumbrous pulpit has more the appearance of a conventicle than a church'. In 1841 the industrialist Sir John Morris, who held the advowson or right of patronage, sold it for £2,500 to the Church Patronage Society. This was an Evangelical body, closely linked to the Church Pastoral Aid Society, and utilized its patronage through the medium of trusts. The arrangement ensured that the clergy appointed to St. Mary's were evangelical and Protestant in their churchmanship and should also have ensured that the clergy appointed to daughter churches, when the parish was broken up, would be similarly minded. St. Mary's tended to set the theological tone of churchmanship throughout the two deaneries of Gower. The established church was not the only shaper of theological opinion in the area. Dissent in all its forms had taken early and deep root within the town, in a number of the smaller parishes of peninsular Gower and within the increasingly industrial parishes of Llangyfelach, Llangiwg and Llansamlet. The Religious Census of 1851 was to show that Nonconformity had overhauled the Church in its membership numbers and in the number of seats it was able to provide for worshippers. Anyone who trawls through the columns of the *Cambrian* newspaper in the third quarter of the century will detect a widespread antipathy towards Roman Catholicism and a growing suspicion of 'creeping ritualism' within the established church. Ritualists received short shrift from correspondents in the *Cambrian*. One was described as 'an out-and-out Puseyite, a wholesale dealer in histrionics and candles'.

The Building and Dedication of St. Paul's

In 1847 Henry Hussey Vivian married Jessie Dalrymple Goddard, daughter of one of his father's friends who was M.P. for Wiltshire. The wedding took place on the 15th April 1847 at Swindon. She was, wrote J.D.W. in an article on Sketty in the *Herald of Wales* (14th Feb. 1931) 'a sweetly pretty woman and during her lifetime, very short alas! made a stylish picture whilst handling her elegant phaeton and pair of roan ponies along the Sketty roads'. She died on 28th February 1848, aged twenty-two, ten months after the marriage and seventeen days after giving birth to their son Ernest Ambrose. Henry Hussey was inconsolable and recorded 'the blight which has fallen on me and the blessing which still remains'. It was this tragedy which prompted Hussey and his father, John Henry, to build St. Paul's church as a tribute to her memory. It was to combine the functions of an estate church and a family mausoleum. The cost of building was to be shared equally between father and son. Before a start could be made with the building, however, much had to be discussed with the bishop, the Church Commissioners, the Church Patronage Society and the Revd. E.B. Squire, vicar of St. Mary's.

Church extension was to be the watchword of the established church at this time – a movement to win back for the church the ground it had lost to the Nonconformists, by erecting new churches in outlying, populous areas. But the proposed church at Sketty was not a particularly good example of purposeful church extension, for Sketty was no more than a small village at a cross-roads, not a heavy concentration of suburban housing. Squire, had he the resources, would surely have identified more pressing priorities nearer home. The new church was purely a Vivian initiative carried through with the rather grudging cooperation of the vicar of St. Mary's.

There were disagreements over the boundaries of the new chapelry. Mr. Holland, one of the members of the evangelical trust which exercised the patronage of St. Mary's, considered the boundaries proposed by the Vivians 'too extended particularly towards the town'. Mr. Squire, after driving round the district with John Henry Vivian and inspecting the parish maps, suggested a new boundary to which J.H. Vivian assented, subject to his son's approval, which was duly given. The subsequent boundaries of the chapelry set out in the *London Gazette* deserve to be quoted because, apart from their intrinsic interest, they show that the Sketty landscape was still rural, devoid of suburban street development, punctuated here and there by solitary farm houses and residences of the well-to-do which served as reference points in the description.

'The district chapelry of Sketty is bounded on the south by the sea, on the west by the parishes of Oystermouth and Bishopstone, on the north-west by the parishes of Llanrhidian and Loughor, and on the north and east by the remaining part of the said parish of Swansea, from which the said district chapelry is separated by the following line of demarcation – from the north-west point of the lower division of the parish of Swansea, continguous to the parish of Loughor, and south of the field marked in the Parish Tythe Commutation Map No. 38, then following the boundary of the lower division along the road to the point between fields numbered 309 and 474; leaving the boundary of the lower division, and entering the higher division, it follows the road in a north-easterly direction, passing by Cefn Coed and the Cocket, as far as a farm-house situated on the east point of a field No. 1439, which forms the eastern extent of the district. From this along a road running about south-west, and passing round where four roads meet, east of a small triangular plot, No. 1460, situated between the four roads, then following this road, running easterly about two hundred yards to the north-west entrance to Glanmoor. From this point the boundary is marked by the course of a small stream which runs westward of Glanmoor, and eastward of Parkwern grounds, and between fields marked 1463, 1469, 1474, 1479, 1504, 1503, 1502, and 1501, on the west, and 1465, 1464, 1468, 1475, 1478, and 1505, on the east of its course. At this point the stream runs into the reservoir. From the reservoir the boundary is formed by the road which passes the Upper Mill and Bryn Mill, to the point on the beach marked "Boundary of the Franchise" on the map aforesaid, from which all the numbers herein mentioned are taken, as such district chapelry of Sketty is more particularly delineated on the map or plan hereunto annexed, and thereon coloured green.'

St. Mary's was to be compensated for loss of fees with a payment of £300.

Given the theological and ecclesiological opinions Henry Hussey Vivian had formed at Trinity College, it was natural that he should have invited an ecclesiologist to design St. Paul's. He chose Henry Woodyer (1816-96), the friend and first pupil of William Butterfield. Butterfield had already completed his plans for All Saint's, Margaret Street, which was to become the flagship of the Anglo-Catholic cause in the west end of London. St. Paul's, Sketty was, of course, built on a more modest scale. But it was Woodyer's reputation as Butterfield's pupil and Woodyer's membership of the Ecclesiological Society to which he was elected in 1848, which drew John Mason Neale to visit Swansea and report on his new church. The church was not quite finished but Neale wrote a favourable critique, (with one or two obvious errors), and it appeared before the church's consecration in *The Ecclesiologist*, XI (1850), p.145:

> *S. David, Sketley [sic], Gower, in Glamorganshire* – We have to congratulate Mr. Woodyer on a very successful village church: indeed, for situation, character, and detail, taken conjointly, we could not easily point to a better example. It consists of well developed chancel, south chapel to chancel, south aisle to nave, south porch, western tower. The style is Middle-Pointed. The east window has three lights; the two to the north of the chancel two lights, all good. On the south are two equal shafted sedilia, and to their west a plain and good door, through which, by steps, you descend into a sacristy, abutting on the south chapel. The east window of this chapel, above the lean-to, is a spherical triangle, and on the south are two cinqfoiled lancets. The nave has, on the north side, one window of three, and two of two lights: the effect is irregular and pleasing. On its south side are four good Middle-Pointed piers, free and bold, with two responds. The south windows of the aisle are, one of four, two of two lights. The belfry arch is good and plain, without capitals. The tower, with stone spire, not quite finished, is very pretty; the latter perhaps a thought heavy. Of the internal fittings we cannot speak, as the building was only just roofed-in when we saw it. The roof, without having any particular fault, pleased us least. We hope that so very good a church will not be disfigured by the want of a screen. The porch was scarcely commenced. The stones employed are Bath and Painswick. We would call Mr. Woodyer's attention to the capabilities of the local *Nolton.*

Neale gave the incorrect dedication, St. David instead of St. Paul, and he should have noted that the main stone used was the local Pennant sandstone with Bath stone ashlar dressings. The critique was written in a hurry for Neale had been intrigued by a lecture which E.A. Freeman had delivered to the Cambrian Archaeological Association in 1849 on the

Gower churches and wished to visit some of them before returning home. The reporter in the *Cambrian* used the account from the *Ecclesiologist* but added valuable additional material particularly on the furnishings. The church was 97 feet long and 37 feet wide and provided accommodation for three hundred and fifty persons, and if the second, north aisle were added, for five hundred. The eastern window, by Warrington, was the gift of Mrs. Vivian and the two lights of the window to the north of the chancel were handsomely stained. The south chapel, mentioned in the *Ecclesiologist* and *Cambrian* became the Vivian chapel, a mortuary chapel beneath which was the family vault. The piers which carried the arcades between nave and south aisle had capitals with ball flower ornament. An arch led into the basement of the tower into which was placed the fine font, the gift of Mrs. Sarah Leves (1792-1868) [not Levies as the *Cambrian* states] who acted as friend and nurse to the Vivian family for thirty-five years. It is an octagonal font, the upper panels of the bowl being decorated with sculpted traceried windows. The lower sloping stem has sculpted windows without panes. Above the basement of the tower was the square belfry containing a peal of eight bells in F cast by Messrs. Mears of London. The tenor weighed 15 cwt. and all were composed of the finest copper and tin especially prepared at the Hafod works. The tower supported a broach-spire, that is, one carried from a square base into an octagonal section by means of triangular faces. Covered with shingle, it rose to a height of 120 feet and formed a conspicuous landmark. The ringers were trained by Mr. Ebbels of St. Mary's, Swansea. The organ occupied a loft above the vestry and had a gallery above the sedilia overlooking the high altar. Made by Mr. Walker of London, the organ had sixteen stops and was the gift of Mr. and Mrs. Dillwyn of Hendrefoilan. The pulpit, then on the north side, was of oak. So too were the low-backed benches fitted with doors for the congregation, and the stalls for the choir. The Communion plate was the joint gift of Mrs. Eden and the Revd. John Eden, Mrs. Webber and Capt. Lindsay. The books, designed by Woodyer, were presented by Mr. Thos. Edward Thomas and his family. The nave had a cusped arch-braced roof and the chancel a scissor-braced roof. The church was built under the provisions of the church building acts of 1818, 1824 and 1843 (Peel's Act) and the living was endowed by the Vivian family with £40 per annum and the income arising from pew rents: as the Revd. Roger Brown has noted, 'a rather uncertain source of income for a man who wished to be independent in his ministry'. To acquire the patronage of St. Paul's from St. Mary's, J.H. Vivian had erected a vicarage in Walter Road for the vicar of St. Mary's and it was occupied by him and his successors until Brooklands was acquired.

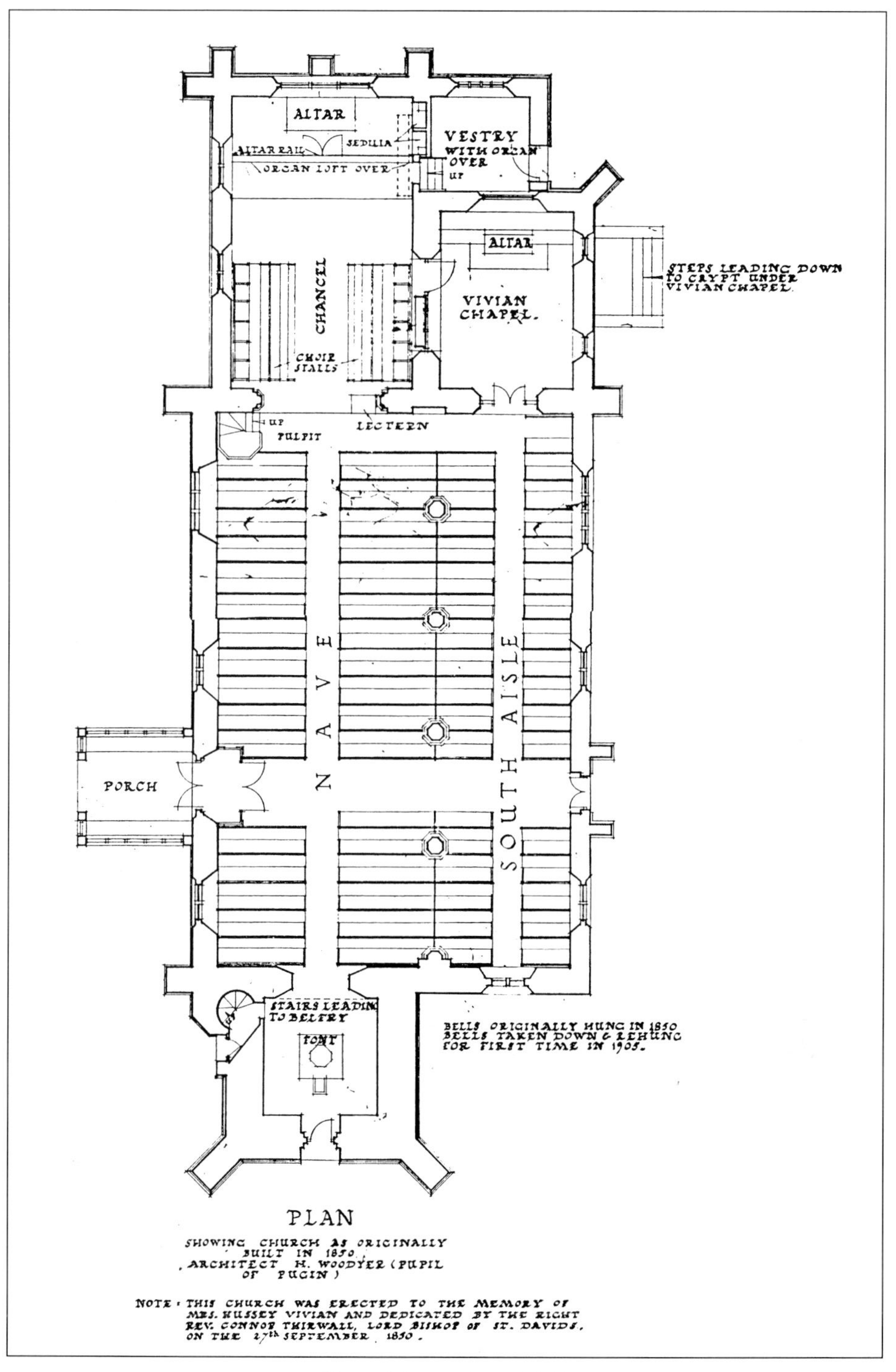

Plan of St. Paul's, *c.*1850

(St. Paul's Church Archives/West Glamorgan Record Office)

Such was the church which Connop Thirlwall, bishop of St. David's, had come to Swansea to consecrate. He arrived on Thursday 26th September 1850. The documents connected with the endowment fund and other formal matters were signed at St. Mary's vestry by the vicar, Revd. E.B. Squire in the presence of J.H. Vivian, Henry Hussey Vivian, the two churchwardens and the bishop. The bishop was then taken to dinner at Singleton where he spent the night. The consecration took place on the following day, 27th September. The church was already full, well before service time, with forty clergy from the dioceses of St. David's and Llandaff in attendance. The bishop was received at the entrance and a petition, read by Valentine Davies, registrar of the diocese, was presented to him requesting that he consecrate the church. He then processed with the clergy and returned singing the 24th Psalm: 'The Earth is the Lord's, and all that therein is: the compass of the world, and they that dwell therein'. The bishop took his seat at the north side of the Communion table and was presented with the instruments of donation and endowment which were duly signed. The consecration service followed and ended with Chancellor Melville reading the 'Sentence of consecration' which was signed by the bishop. The preliminary prayers of the Communion service were then read by the Revd. E.A. Sanford, the first incumbent of St. Paul's, the lessons by the vicar of Swansea, the epistle and gospel by the Chancellor and rural dean and the Commandments and Nicene creed by the bishop. The bishop preached the sermon on a text from Psalm 116, verses 12, 13, 14: 'What shall I render unto the Lord for all his benefits towards me? I will take the cup of salvation, and call upon the name of the Lord. I will pay my vows unto the Lord now in the presence of all his people.' Its theme was gratitude to God. The bishop, clergy and a large part of the congregation then repaired to the churchyard for its consecration and returned to the church for the completion of the Communion service.

The service in the afternoon took place at 4 p.m. when the vicar of Swansea read the prayers and the Revd. Samuel Davies, rural dean and perpetual curate of Oystermouth, read the lessons. The Revd. E.A. Sanford, the new incumbent preached, taking as his text St. Paul's Epistle to the Corinthians, chapter 14, verse 15: 'I will pray with the spirit, and I will pray with the understanding also'. The gist of the sermon was that all prayer, in whatever form it is offered, is acceptable to God but that very many weighty reasons existed for a set form of prayer as set out in the liturgy of the Book of Common Prayer, 'which had preserved pure doctrine through the dark ages, while other churches not possessing a liturgy, had fallen into error during those periods'. The

St. Paul's, *c.*1850
(St. Paul's Church Archives/West Glamorgan Record Office)

sermon bore all the hall marks of a good Tractarian, a disciple of the Oxford Movement.

For the first four months or so of its existence St. Paul's was a chapel of ease to St. Mary's but on 3rd February 1851 an Order in Council issued under the auspices of the Ecclesiastical Commissioners gave St. Paul's separate ecclesiastical status as 'The District Chapelry of Sketty'. It was now a new, autonomous parish.

Early Incumbents

The first incumbent of St. Paul's was the Revd. Edward A. Sanford (the *Cambrian* correctly spells his name thus though it was later rendered as Sandford). He was, like his two successors, licenced by the bishop as a *perpetual curate*, not inducted and instituted as a *vicar*. J.A. Venn who listed the *alumni* of Cambridge colleges, describes him as a sizar of St. John's and a ten year man. A sizar was an undergraduate who received a grant from his College to assist in paying his expenses. A sizar was formerly expected to perform certain menial services later undertaken by college servants and received his *sizings* (allowances of food) free. As a ten year man he was allowed, provided he was over twenty-four years of age and had kept his name on the college boards for ten years, to proceed B.D. on payment of certain fees. The *Cambrian* helpfully adds the information that he had been 'a college friend at Cambridge of Mr. Hussey Vivian'. Sanford was ordained deacon and priest in 1846 and was already thirty-two years of age when he came to Sketty. He held the living from September 1850 to November 1851 when he took up the living of Combe Florey in Somersetshire on the presentation of the Lord Chancellor.

His successor was the Revd. Montague Earle Welby, a member of a well-to-do Leicestershire family known to the Vivians. Born on 17th December 1827, he was the fourth son of the Revd. John Earle Welby, rector of Harston, Leics., the grandson of Sir William Earle Welby, first baronet, and brother of Lord Welby and of Felicia Lady Lindsey. He was educated at Eton and Magdalen College, Oxford, of which he was a

Revd. M. E. Welby with members of choir
(South Wales Evening Post, 29.11.1939)

demy (that is, a foundation scholar whose allowance or 'commons' was originally half that of a Fellow). He graduated in 1851, took his M.A. in 1851 and was a Fellow of his college between 1851 and 1853. He was ordained deacon by Dr. Samuel Wilberforce, bishop of Oxford in 1851 and priest by Dr. Connop Thirlwall, bishop of St. David's in the same year.

The memory of Welby's early clerical career has been kept alive in the diary of Francis Kilvert who described his appearance and quirks of character in 1870, only three years after he had left Swansea, when he undertook a locum for Mr. Venables, the rector of Clyro. 'He is,' writes Kilvert, 'a pleasant-looking, pleasant-mannered man with good features but with a light lackadaisical inconsequent unstable air . . . is rather given to light clerical slang and playfully alludes to his gown as his 'black' which he did not much approve of preaching in. He brought his own robes to church in a bundle and wore a cassock in which I should think he must have been uncommonly cold sitting in the chancel'. He was a good preacher. 'Mrs. Baskerville,' writes Kilvert, 'said she had heard that a lady had been carried out of Hay church fainting under the influence of a sermon from Mr. Welby. The story is probably untrue'. He was an expert fund raiser and succeeded in rebuilding the church of Llanlleonfel within little over a year of becoming its vicar. He had also acquired a 'following'. Kilvert refers to his own firm friend Mrs. Brewer 'who is staunch to us and does not run after Mr. Welby like most people'.

All these characteristics must have been familiar to his parishioners at Sketty. He enthusiastically joined in the evangelical and social work of the Dillwyns of Hendrefoilan House in the Dunvant-Killay area and as a result formed an attachment to Mary Dillwyn, daughter of Lewis Weston Dillwyn, the owner of the Cambrian Pottery. He married her at St. Paul's on 13th August 1857. The *Cambrian* newspaper shows him taking an active part in the social and ecclesiastical life of Swansea and its neighbourhood, preaching and fund raising for local charities and serving on the committees for social betterment so beloved of the Victorians. He also took a confirmation class at the Swansea Grammar school and the Revd. Roger Brown recounts in a recent, as yet unpublished, article how Welby told them something about Connop Thirlwall, the bishop who was to confirm them. They were more impressed by the fact that he ate five boiled eggs for breakfast than that he had been a senior wrangler at Cambridge (i.e. one who had secured the highest class in the mathematical tripos). Canon D.T.W. Price, who has also chronicled Welby's clerical career in some detail, has suggested, almost certainly correctly, that he was a high churchman because several of the parishes he subsequently served had a Tractarian tradition.

But there was another side to his character. His substantial private income – his estate was valued at £67,851 when he died on 31st December 1910 – made him something of a law unto himself. On a number of occasions he absented himself from the parish without informing the churchwardens and without making any provision for the Sunday services. A small bundle of letters has survived in the parish records which show how concerned the churchwardens were about these unauthorised absences. In one undated letter, Iltid Thomas of Hill House, the People's warden, warned Welby that 'a recurrence will compel me as churchwarden to lay the whole matter before the bishop'. Hussey Vivian, the incumbent's warden, took the trouble to look up the legislation on clerical absenteeism, had it copied and passed on to Iltid. Here is Welby writing to Iltid Thomas after receiving a ticking off from Hussey Vivian. The letter is undated but was most probably sent sometime in 1854 and is addressed from Radbourne Hall, near Derby: 'Hussey Vivian has written me about the services. Indeed, I have been very negligent but I'm sure you will forgive me. The deep affliction through which I have lately passed [a family bereavement] has been absorbing my thought till I forgot all besides. However I am better now – change of scene and place has recruited my spirits and time as it passes cleans (?) off the keener edge of sorrow. Tomorrow I believe there is to be one full service – and I hope to be back at Sketty by the following Sunday when I will give prayers in the morning. Remember me most kindly to Mrs. Iltid.' There are a number of postscripts. 'Of course when I am away the church must be closed unless a clergyman kindly volunteers his services. The incumbent of St. Paul's does not get £100 per annum. The congregation would hardly I suppose treat me so shabbily as to expect me to pay 3 or 4 guineas each Sunday for services. I am not stationary so do not write.' And here is Hussey writing to Iltid from London: 'I return enclosed Welby's letter to me: we have managed to get him straight and I hope he will keep so. I am very glad you spoke out clearly and firmly on the matter, as he might have fancied I was solitary in my views of his behaviour. What an odd compound he is.' Trouble recurred in July 1861 when the congregation assembled at 11 a.m. and after waiting until 11.20 a.m. 'and no clergyman appearing or likely to appear the congregation dispersed'. The parishioners were naturally indignant but Welby still managed to retain a 'following' at Sketty who lamented his move to Oystermouth on his appointment as perpetual curate there in 1865. A parishioner signing himself O.P.Q., Rose Cottage, Sketty wrote to the *Cambrian* (27.1.65) 'With regret I hear we are on the eve of losing our esteemed pastor. The loss of so kind, pious and charitable friend and gentleman I am certain will be felt by all classes. I therefore hope that all his friends and neighbours will be up and doing to present him with a Testimonial, as he deserves.' According to the Revd. E.G. Williams in his pamphlet *Move On*, Welby had become dissatisfied with Sketty and this prompted his move to Oystermouth.

Revd. E.W. Bolney 1865-1903

Welby was succeeded as perpetual curate by Edward William Brown who changed his name to Bolney in November 1868 to comply with the legal requirements of a legacy from his aunt. Born in 1840 at Stamford, Lincs., he was admitted a pensioner (the equivalent of a commoner at Oxford) at Trinity College, Cambridge in 1859 and graduated B.A. in 1863 (M.A. 1867). He was appointed Vice-Principal of the South Wales Training College, Carmarthen and ordained deacon in 1864 and priest in 1865 (St. David's diocese). Bolney's long incumbency at Sketty was a particularly memorable one because he acquired a Boswell of sorts in the person of James Pugsley (1861-1929). Pugsley was a member of a well-known family of Swansea ecclesiastical decorators and ended his own career as an L.M.S. railway official at Victoria Station, Swansea. He became a chorister at St. Paul's in the 1870s and appears as a young man in the celebrated photograph of the choir in 1877. He gained a reputation as an historian of the local churches, interested himself in church controversies and was a contributor to the local press. His most valuable contributions to church history are *Reminiscences of definite church progress in Swansea and neighbourhood during the last twenty years* (Swansea, 1906) and a revised and enlarged edition *Church life and thought in Swansea and the neighbourhood* (Swansea, 1915). He was an Anglo-Catholic, a member of its semi-official mouth piece, the English Church Union, but in the last years of his life was shocked by what he considered Anglo-Catholic excesses at St. Gabriel's, Brynmill.

In his younger days, prior to the erection of Christ Church (1872) Pugsley considered St. Paul's as 'the only parish for miles around in which the services of the church were conducted in anything approaching Prayer Book order and churchmen of the "Catholic" school of thought in the church . . . made Sketty their spiritual oasis, in the barren land of Protestantism where no water was'. However, it would be wrong to imply that the services at Sketty had assumed Anglo-Catholic proportions. Although Bolney prided himself on being 'an old fashioned high churchman of the Gladstonian type', Averil Stewart, Henry Hussey's granddaughter, records that churchmanship at Sketty was 'broad rather than

Expenses of St. Paul's, Sketty.

	£	s.	d.
Cleaning Church	5	0	0
Stove	3	0	0
Organ Blower	1	0	0
Surplice	2	12	6
Wine	2	10	0
Lighting	4	14	3
Sundries	2	0	11
Books for Choir	0	17	4
	21	15	0
Interest on Legacy left by late J. H. Vivian, Esq.	12	5	4
Deficit	9	9	8

The above Expenses will be felt by the Congregation to be simply those necessarily incidental to Divine Worship. They have heretofore been deducted from the Stipend of the Incumbent, but it will be felt that they ought properly to be borne by the congregation, and we have consequently suggested that a collection should be made to meet them.

H. HUSSEY VIVIAN,
ILTID THOMAS. } Churchwardens

Easter, 1866.

Church expenses, 1866
(St. Paul's Church Archives/West Glamorgan Record Office)

low certainly not high'. Fortunately, Pugsley describes in some detail the nature of the services and the way they were conducted during Bolney's incumbency.

The Sunday morning service consisted of what Pugsley calls 'a trinity of offices rolled into one': Morning Prayer, Litany and Ante Communion to the end of the Nicene Creed with sermon. This was the Anglican equivalent of the pre-Reformation and post-Reformation Roman Catholic Dry Mass. On the first and third Sunday in each month the service was completed with the full Communion service and the sermon dropped. On these Communion Sundays a general exodus occurred after the Nicene Creed 'leaving the one service of Our Lord's institution', writes Pugsley, 'to be celebrated to comparatively empty benches'. In response to an urgent appeal from leading residents, the hour on the third Sunday was changed from 11 a.m. to 8.30 a.m. and this new celebration was branded by some church, as well as non-church people, as an imitation of the Roman Mass. Holy days were regularly observed with Morning Prayer and Ante-Communion while Lent was marked with services on Wednesday and Friday, and Holy Week with daily services.

St. Paul's was the first to use the Lenten metrical litanies and among the first to adopt *Hymns Ancient and Modern* (1861), which was regarded with suspicion as 'Puseyite' when it first appeared. Bolney celebrated in cassock, surplice, hood and black stole, 'the latter having the three embroidered golden crosses on the neck and both ends, probably again the only clergyman in the whole of the district to wear the sacred symbol on any portion of his ministerial attire, or even to appear in a cassock, which was then considered nothing better than a 'monkish petticoat', while the general use of a correctly shaped stole of whatever colour was utterly unknown.' Bolney adopted the eastward position in his early years at Sketty but abandoned it after the Purchas judgment of the Privy Council had declared it illegal in 1871. Thereafter he adopted the 'north end' position, as indeed did Archbishop Frederick Temple (d.1902) and, Pugsley might have added, John Henry Newman throughout his Anglican career. Yet Bolney put no obstacle in the way of visiting priests using the eastward position. The altar in Bolney's day was sparsely adorned. It had a retable (a sort of pedestal at the rear surface of the altar), on which rested a rather sombre cross 'unadorned with gilt or any brilliant substance – an ornament of this description would have aroused strong opposition at this time'. It was replaced in 1886/7 by one of brass when the surpliced choir was introduced. The cross was flanked by vases of flowers. Bolney, writes Pugsley, never pandered to the widely prevalent custom of evening communion (though Welby had done so). Nor did he try to exalt preaching into the dignity of a sacrament. He showed courage in inviting Berdmore Compton, the Anglo-Catholic vicar of All Saints, Margaret St. to celebrate at St. Paul's during the first Church Congress held in Swansea in 1879. Compton had been a forceful opponent of the Public Worship Regulation Act, 1874 which Hussey Vivian, Bolney's patron, had enthusiastically supported in the Commons (see below).

The choir stalls were not at first occupied by a surpliced choir. The men in the choir wore their ordinary suits and the boys wore a 'livery' introduced by Mrs. Sarah Vivian, wife of John Henry Vivian (d.1855). It consisted of dark grey trousers, black Eton jackets, with linen collar, black silk necktie and red and black check waistcoat of Welsh flannel. The size of the check was varied from year to year so that Mrs. Vivian

St. Paul's Choir, 1877
Jno. Edwards, Wm. Edwards, D. Edwards, J. Edwards, J. Evans, J. Gwyn, T. Gwyn.
Phil Gwyn, Thos. Gwyn, Dd. Williams, J. Pugsley.
Joe Gwyn, W. Chamberlain, W. Kneath, F. Williams, T. Mathews, Mr. Cryer (Orgt.),
J. Wright, J. Hoskins, W. Brown, S. Franks, J. Thomas.
(St. Paul's Church Archives/West Glamorgan Record Office)

would know they were wearing their new suits. She had designed the livery because she thought Hussey had looked smart when he wore a similar outfit at Eton and because she thought the surplice a popish garment. The choir boys probably disliked the livery – they were jeered by the non-church boys as 'Robin redbreasts' and 'Sketty robins'. The dress was continued until the death of Sarah Vivian in 1886 'when it was discarded at the instance of the late Lord Swansea, and the more reverent and becoming surplice took its place'.

Meanwhile Bolney had acquired a new title. As we have seen, he had been licenced and appointed to St. Paul's as a perpetual curate. The office had a complex history which one need not examine here. It was not completely abolished in the Church of England until 1969. The title of the office was universally disliked by those who held it and was felt to be a badge of ignomy. As E.A. Freeman observed in the *Saturday Review* (9th Jan. 1869 p.45), 'Perpetual curate sounded as painfully like "once a curate and always a curate".' In 1868 Parliament enacted that 'the incumbent of every parish or new parish . . . not being a rector, who is . . . authorised to publish banns of matrimony . . . and to solemnize therein marriages, churchings and baptisms . . . and who is entitled to take the entire fees arising from such offices . . . shall, for the purpose of style and designation be deemed and styled the vicar'. Parson Bolney could now refer to himself as vicar and did indeed do so.

Of far greater importance for the future history of St. Paul's, however, was the radical change which had taken place in the views which the patron, Henry Hussey Vivian, held of the Church of England and of the high church party within it. What prompted the change is still a matter for speculation but the *volte-face* was certainly complete by 1874. In that year Disraeli's second ministry introduced the Public Worship Regulation Bill. It aimed at crushing ritualism in the Church of England by giving parishioners the power (subject to the sanction of the bishop) to prosecute a clergyman for ritualistic practices. On 22nd July C.R.M. Talbot's son Theodore, an ardent Anglo-Catholic, wrote a long letter to Hussey urging him not to support the bill when it came to the Commons. Theodore, writing at some length to justify his own views, urged Hussey to oppose the measure on the grounds of liberty, toleration and fair play 'which must ever be the platform of the real Liberal party'. Hussey had carefully read the text of the bill and had followed the debates in the Lords. Even after reading Theodore's letter he now decided to give the bill his whole-hearted support. 'Church matters have, as you may know,' he wrote to Theodore, 'much occupied my thoughts for upwards of thirty years. At first I was attracted to High Church views and practice but I very soon saw their extreme danger and since that time, without being either a High, Low or Broad churchman, I have endeavoured to hold to what I believe are the true doctrines and practice of the Church of England.'

Meanwhile the publication of an Anglo-Catholic manual on confession *The Priest in Absolution* had caused a flurry of protest in London. It prompted Sir William Harcourt to write to the *Times* and warn of the dangers of such a practice as an intrusion into family life, citing the boast of a Spanish Confessor to the King of Spain, 'I hold your God in my hand, and I have your wife at my feet'. The volume published originally in two parts (1866 and 1870) was by this time (1877) circulating outside the ranks of the clergy. Henry Hussey was shown a copy by C.R.M. Talbot and went down to the Commons in high dudgeon to ask the government 'to take such legal steps as may be necessary to ascertain the names of any clergymen of the Church of England who may be members of the Society of the Holy Cross' (the publishers of the volume) 'and to take further steps . . . so as to effectively prevent such clergymen from continuing to minister within the pale of the church against the doctrines, disciplines and practice of which they are declared to be in conspiracy . . .'

And on and on. Hussey could be effortlessly pompous when he chose, as that good judge of character Amy Dillwyn noted. Hussey had been in his younger days a friend of Friedrich Engels (joint author with Karl Marx of the Communist Manifesto) but Marx labelled him 'Bourgeois Vivian' and poked fun at his naivety in *Das Kapital.*

By 1885 Hussey considered himself a Christian first and a churchman second and claimed to have laid the foundation stones of more nonconformist chapels than any man alive. Why, he asked in a speech in support of disestablishment in that year, were church attendances falling? The answer partly lay in the new-fangled practices introduced by some young and indiscreet incumbent which offended their Protestant feelings. Had it not been for the great orthodox nonconformist bodies, he argued, this country would have been sunk in the depths of heathendom. He now launched an attack on the doctrine of the apostolic succession. It was not, he claimed, a doctrine of the Church of England, not in her articles of faith, creeds or canons but was 'a noxious relic of superstition and priestcraft and the main barrier between church and dissent'. Confession and absolution were the natural fruits of this doctrine.

How far Hussey's change of views led him to interfere in the services at St. Paul's is difficult to say. Averil Stewart records that on one occasion a new (visiting?) parson turned to the east at the creed. Vivian stepped out from his pew, remarked 'we don't do that here' and turned him around again. Yet Pugsley's account of practice at St. Paul's contradicts this. Averil Stewart was critical of Bolney's sermons which 'were of singular length and extremely dull. Worse, he sprayed rather than prayed so that those beneath the pulpit [then on the north side overlooking the Vivian pew] wished they had brought umbrellas'. Amy Dillwyn also disliked Bolney's mode of conducting the services – he read the lessons far too slowly, mumbling them into his whiskers when he ought to have intoned them in the proper Church of England manner. He took her advice but was later remembered for intoning the church notices as well. On another celebrated occasion Averil Stewart records that Henry Hussey, seated in the front row of the church after arduous weeks of canvassing for the Liberal cause before the General Election of 1892 heard the parson (Bolney?) tell the congregation 'that he believed our Saviour to have been a Progressive Conservative'. He nearly walked out. Gladstone's visit to Swansea in 1889 was a political and municipal rather than an ecclesiastical event but his attendance at Sketty church for the Sunday services on 5th June was long remembered. Accompanied by Hussey, Lord Aberdare, two M.P.s and others, he walked across the park from Singleton Abbey into the churchyard. The gate has gone but the avenue leading to

Revd. E. W. Bolney
(St. Paul's Church Archives/West Glamorgan Record Office)

it is still marked by surviving trees and referred to as Gladstone's Way. Canon J. Allan Smith, vicar of St. Mary's, preached at the 11 a.m. and Bolney at the 6.30 p.m. service. Gladstone entered in his diary: 'Church 11 a.m. – notable sermon and Holy Communion (service long). Again 6½ p.m. – good sermon'.

Despite rather unkind censures from some of the leaders of Sketty society, Bolney was well-loved by the people of Sketty for his kindness, charity and sincerity and for the boundless hospitality he dispensed at his bachelor home to members of church organisations especially at Christmas time. His was a familiar figure around Sketty village for he walked with a limp and his long beard was white even when he was fifty. He retired in 1903 after serving St. Paul's for over forty-five years and died at his home at Eaton Grove on 2nd May 1906. Parishioners erected a marble plaque on the south wall of the chancel to commemorate his long vicariate.

Henry Hussey Vivian, *c.* 1885
(St. Paul's Church Archives/West Glamorgan Record Office)

Revd. C.G.C. Lillingston (1903-08) and Revd. D. Akrill-Jones (1909-15)

Had Henry Hussey lived to see Bolney's retirement in 1903 he would undoubtedly have exercised his patronage to appoint a low churchman to St. Paul's. John Aubrey, born in 1854, was the only son of Hussey's second marriage to Caroline Elizabeth Cholmeley in 1853. (The marriage ended with her death in 1868 after a long period of illness). He remained Hussey's 'greatest comfort' yet developed religious views diametrically opposed to his father's. He was a devout Tractarian, and Anglo-Catholic and a member of the English Church Union. His bound, annotated copies of the *Tracts for the Times* now rest on the library shelves of University of Wales, Swansea. He was of too retiring a nature to have exercised any influence on the choice of a successor to Bolney, and had in any case died in 1898. The exercise of the Vivian patronage fell to Hussey's younger brother William Graham Vivian, the last surviving trustee of his father's will. He was, if anything, more radically Protestant and rabidly anti-

Catholic than his brother and appointed the evangelical Cecil George Campbell Lillingston to the living. Any hopes which Bolney might have entertained that St. Paul's would continue as a moderate centre of Tractarian practice had been dashed and it may be significant that during his retirement he worshipped at St. Gabriel's which was already moving away from its evangelical beginnings and adopting, to use Pugsley's words, 'definite Catholic teaching and practice'.

Lillingston had entered Hertford College, Oxford as an Exhibitioner and took a 3rd class in History moderations and graduated B.A. in 1894. He went for his ministerial training to Wycliffe Hall, was ordained deacon in1896 and priest in 1897. Before coming to St. Paul's he had served curacies at Huddersfield and Brompton, London and was acting chaplain to the Forces in South Africa, 1901-3. The evangelical regime he introduced at St. Paul's was heartily disliked by James Pugsley. Like his hero Bolney, Pugsley preferred 'the steady-going type of Christianity to spasmodic outbursts of emotion, and loud sounding phrases of conversion . . .

Revd. C. G. C. Lillingston
(St. Paul's Church Archives/West Glamorgan Record Office)

of being warm one day and cold the next'. Lillingston had dropped the so-called Athanasian creed although it had been in use at St. Paul's for over thirty-eight years and its recitation on certain feast days was ordered by a rubric in the Prayer Book. This creed had been a source of controversy in the Anglican church since the 1860s because of its condemnatory clauses and readers of Kilvert's diary will remember him at Ilston rectory sitting up until 1 o'clock disputing about the creed, Bolney 'taking the high church ground and Westhorp and I the liberal view . . .' Lillingston now ceased to support the Society for the Propagation of the Gospel in Foreign Parts (the oldest missionary society of the Church of England) and favoured instead evangelical societies such as the Church Missionary Society and the Colonial and Continental Church Society. He had also given his support to the 'United Undenominational Open Air' and other meetings, as well as to the Young Women's Christian Association which are, writes Pugsley peevishly, 'scarcely to be considered as feeders or hand maidens of our church'.

After these grumbles, however, Pugsley had grudgingly to admit that no material changes had been made in the outward character of the general services. Altar cross, flowers and frontals had been retained and orientation at the Apostles and Nicene creeds observed. Additional services had been introduced: weekly and saints day celebrations of Holy Communion and Wednesday evening services. The church was opened daily for private prayer. The psalms and responses were now chanted at Morning and Evening Prayer. Cassocks were donned for the first time by members of the choir as under-garments for their surplices. A parish hall had been erected in October 1906 for mission services and meetings (the hall on Gower Rd. above Sketty Cross, is now used by the Seventh Day Adventists).

Pugsley might have added other achievements to Lillingston's credit. The great spiritual revival that was apparent in the parish at this time owed much to him. During the first months of his ministry he had visited every family in the village. He organised Bible classes in groups under class leaders, started or rather re-started the Mothers' Union at Sketty, introduced the monthly parish magazine in January 1905 and was among the first local churchmen to exhibit a truly ecumenical outlook. At a more material level he had the north aisle built (see below), the heating system refurbished, the bells rehung and collected £800 towards the building of a new vicarage. He also inaugurated the Church Council in 1906, 'a body through which the opinion of the congregation could be voiced'. To him has been attributed the maxim 'where there is no prayer in the pew there is no power in the pulpit'.

Lillingston left St. Paul's in December 1908 to take up the living of Christ Church, Clifton and died in January 1915 at the early age of forty-three. His successor was David Akrill-Jones. Educated at Merton College, Oxford, he graduated in 1890 and was ordained deacon in 1890 and priest in 1891. After serving curacies in Canton, Newport and Kensington, he was vicar of Prendergast from 1898 to 1909. Akrill-Jones was also an evangelical but was welcomed by Pugsley because 'he reverted, to a great extent, to the older and more definite traditions of this early temple of revised Anglican decency and regularity'. He is perhaps best remembered for the grand bazaar which was held at the Albert Hall to raise funds for a vicarage: 'to help house the poor vicar of Sketty' as the souvenir pamphlet announced. The vicarage was built and eventually became The Old Vicarage residential home near the top Cross. New organisations now appeared in the parish: the Girls Friendly Society, the Church of England Men's Society and the Church Lads Brigade. The Sketty Church Cricket Club founded in 1890 took on a new lease of life under the leadership of the Revd. Norman Parcell, assistant curate.

Akrill-Jones introduced daily Matins and Evensong and an early weekly celebration of Holy Communion. He adopted the eastward in place of the north end position when celebrating the Eucharist. The chief Sunday morning service consisting, as we have seen, of Matins, Litany and Ante-Communion, which had been the custom from 1850 to 1912, was now remodelled and Morning Prayer and sermon as a separate service took its place on the first and third Sundays of the month, followed by a separate celebration of Holy Communion. Matins and Litany was only said on its own on the second, fourth and, when it occurred, on the fifth Sunday of each month. Akrill-Jones resigned his Sketty living to become vicar of Bolsover in 1915.

CHAPTER 2

'Good Anglican Worship of the Middle Way', 1914-50

War, Disestablishment and the Departure of the Vivians

All the niceties of religious observance together with the minutiae of Prayer Book rubrics so beloved by Pugsley began to dissolve into insignificance soon after the outbreak of war with Germany on 4th August 1914. It was the first full-scale continental war Britain had engaged in for a century. Most people predicted a short war – over by Christmas! But as the conflict on the western front developed into a war of attrition and conscription was introduced in 1916, the social and religious life of Sketty changed. The parish was denuded of most of its young men and their absence from the church services and the societies they manned was obvious to all. The emotional impact of the war was felt at its keenest when the names of those who had been killed or maimed were announced in what was still a small village community. The newly constituted Church Council met in the church hall on 23rd January 1914 – the first Council seemed to have fizzled out after its establishment in 1906. By the following year the church hall had been commandeered by the Red Cross and fifteen wounded soldiers were being treated there. The minutes of the Church Council now began to record the deaths of young parishioners on the western front but the minutes unaccountably break off after July 1917 and were not resumed until April 1920. The Revd. Akrill-Jones' two sons were killed and eventually seventy-four Sketty parishioners lost their lives in the conflict.

As a Liberal M.P. Hussey Vivian had supported the movement for disestablishing the Welsh Church. He saw it not only as a fair and just measure but also as a means of combating ritualism and Anglo-Catholicism within the church. 'Disestablishment,' he declared in a speech in 1885, 'must lead to the creation of a governing body, similar to that of the Irish Church, which having a predominance of the lay element, would soon effectively dispose of practices of this nature, and the church would soon cease to be the most effective instrument of Romanising our people.' Most churchmen who were aware of the implications of the Act when it passed through Parliament in 1914, however, feared that it would, by confiscating to secular uses 'endowments consecrated to the service of God', bankrupt the Welsh Church, impede its pastoral mission, isolate it from the mainstream of Anglican life and thought and aid Nonconformist expansion. The fears proved unfounded but were real enough to those who had to prepare the church for the inevitable.

The implementation of the 1914 Act was postponed and pressure to amend it continued; there was even hope that it might be repealed if a Conservative government was returned to power. In April 1914 Akrill-Jones rejoiced 'that 217 of our adult Nonconformist friends in the parish have signified their sympathy with their fellow Christians of our church by freely signing the protest against taking away from us our ancient churchyards and £157,000 a year of our endowments. They are 68 Congregationalists, 58 Wesleyans, 43 Baptists, 20 Methodists, 5 Presbyterians, 2 Roman Catholics, and 20 of other denominations . . . This fact cannot but open our hearts to our brethren, who differ from us in some of their convictions, but are one with us in the spirit. I am sure that, whatever be the issue before us, the outcome of this process will be better understanding and a further step towards Christian unity.' It was a remarkably early statement of ecumenical principles and ideals.

The Act after some amendment came into operation on 1st April 1920. The Welsh bishops were released from their allegiance to the Archbishop of Canterbury and A.G. Edwards, bishop of St. Asaph, was unanimously elected first Archbishop of Wales by his fellow diocesan bishops. Wales became a separate province of the Anglican communion. The Governing Body and the Representative Body were already in position but the full text of the Constitution was not published until April 1922.

Meanwhile the ties which bound the Vivian family to Singleton Abbey and St. Paul's, Sketty, began to loosen and were finally sundered. Henry Hussey Vivian died in 1894, a year after his elevation to the peerage as the first Lord Swansea. His third wife, Averil Beaumont, whom he married in 1870, survived him and lived until 1934. After Hussey's death, William Graham Vivian of Clyne Castle, his younger brother, became head of the family and exercised the patronage of the Sketty living when vicar Bolney died. Graham was an eccentric bachelor who travelled extensively in Europe and entertained lavishly at Clyne Castle which he filled with the art treasures he had collected on his travels. His main interests, according to Hussey, were 'pigeons and flirtation'. Yet he was a shrewd business man, cleverer perhaps than Hussey in dealing with the financial side of the copper smelting business. He died in 1912. Hussey's eldest son, Ernest

Ambrose, 2nd Lord Swansea, had little interest in the copper smelting industry which was already in decline in the latter years of Hussey's life. When George V visited the Hafod Works in 1920, the 2nd Lord Swansea did not make an appearance. He spent his time either travelling or in London, rarely if ever in Singleton. After the fire of 1896 the house looked a sad sight even after some redecoration and rebuilding. A number of Hussey's immediate family had by 1900 left for their house at Cae'r Berys near Builth Wells and in 1901 when Richard Glynn Vivian addressed his poem to the house it was seemingly empty:

> No voice to answer, none to hear me call
> Gone are they all!

In 1919 Ernest Ambrose sold Singleton Abbey and its 254 acre estate to Swansea Corporation. In one Sunday collection at St. Paul's in 1920 the parishioners managed to raise £1,500 towards the £2,500 needed to secure the amenities of the church and enlarge the churchyard. The vacuum left by the departure of the Vivians was soon filled for in 1923 the Corporation gave part of the Vivian estate as the site for the newly-established University College. The ties between the College and St. Paul's, slender at first, were strengthened as the years passed after a succession of its students and staff had worshipped there and members of staff were serving as church officers. The Vivians' connection with industrial Swansea also came to an end. After 1900 the Vivian and Sons Hafod Works amalgamated with the adjoining works of Messrs. Williams Foster and Co. Ltd. and in 1924 both firms were acquired by British Copper Manufacturers Ltd. and this latter company by I.C.I. Ltd. in 1928.

Revd. H.J. Stewart, 1915-41

Such were the major events which formed the background to the early years of Stewart's vicariate. He was offered the living by the Vivian trustees. He hesitated about accepting but 'at the urgent request of Bishop John Owen of St. David's' decided to take on the parish. He was the first incumbent of St. Paul's who was not Oxbridge educated. He graduated with first class honours in History from St. David's College, Lampeter in 1894 and went for his ministerial training to St. Michael's College, then at Aberdare, aptly called by James Pugsley in another context, the 'Cuddeston of Wales'. He was ordained deacon in 1896 and priest in 1897 and served curacies at Llandysul and Llansamlet before spending a year as rector of the Tractarian church of Llangorwen. But Stewart was

Revd. H. J. Stewart
(St. Paul's Church Archives/West Glamorgan Record Office)

not a party man – if anything, he veered to the evangelical wing of the church. He left Llangorwen to become vicar of Cockett (1907-15) and must therefore have been known to the people of Sketty before taking up residence with his wife and two children at what is now the Old Vicarage in February 1915.

He was remembered by one of his successors, Revd. Garfield Hughes James, as 'a sturdy figure with a strong face which gave the impression of a man of sound common sense who has both feet firmly on the ground. He preached well, had a rich voice with something of a crackle in it.' He was a gifted administrator and inevitably in great demand when the church was preparing for disestablishment. It is claimed to be no accident that the initials used (J.S.) in the formulaic texts of solemn declarations embodied in the Constitution are his. Stewart energetically collected in the parish for the Million Pound Fund which was designed to make up for the losses incurred by disendowment and many thousands of pounds were collected. The Fund had reached over £600,000 by 1923.

One of the immediate spin-offs of the Act of Disestablishment was the creation of two new dioceses. The new diocese of Monmouth was formed in 1921. When proposals for the creation of a diocese for Swansea and Brecon came up for discussion in the same year, members of the St. Paul's P.C.C. opposed it as not being opportune as they considered the economy was not buoyant enough to sustain it. Their views were channelled through the ruridecanal conference. Notwithstanding some opposition the new diocese of Swansea and Brecon began its existence on 24th June 1923 and St. Paul's, Sketty with other churches in the old deanery of Gower severed its connection with the diocese of St. David's and found a place in the deanery of Swansea within the newly created archdeaconry of Gower. Stewart was among the first canons created to form the cathedral chapter at Brecon. There were twelve canons, each one taking up residence for one month when funds permitted. Stewart served on the Diocesan Board of Finance and with the consent of the P.C.C. became secretary of the Dilapidations Board of the new diocese under the chairmanship of Charles Eden of Derwen Fawr. This entailed long periods of absence from the parish. During his first Lent at Sketty Stewart with his curate managed to visit all the church people and compile a complete roll of communicants to whom he sent an Easter card. He also, with the help of Stanley Cook, secured a site for allotments below Parc Beck. They are believed to be the first in Swansea and continued in use into the 1980s when they were taken over as a site for new houses.

After the war a building boom began which transformed Sketty into a suburb of Swansea. Visiting this rapidly-growing population now became a problem for the vicar and his curate and they solved it by applying the Derby scheme to the parish. A parishioner would undertake to visit every house in a street or given area and find out who were baptised and confirmed. Details were entered into books which were up-dated in the years following. Stewart was a notable builder. He slated the church spire, built the present vicarage and extended the church chancel, north aisle and vestry area, achievements which will be treated in greater detail in the chapter on fabric and furnishings. It has been estimated that £32,000 was raised for church purposes during his ministry at Sketty.

But perhaps his most memorable achievement was the freeing of the pews. The seating at St. Paul's was in the best traditions of the Ecclesiological Society – benches with low backs giving worshippers in the central area of the church a clear view of the altar and enabling them to use the bench backs in front of them as a support when kneeling. From the earliest days of St. Paul's, however, and in keeping with practice in other Swansea churches, the best seating, up-front and in full view of the altar and within good listening distance of the preacher in the pulpit, was reserved for those who could afford to pay a rent. The poor and less well-to-do were relegated either to the back, with the servants in the south aisle, or to a separate service in the church hall. A plan of the seating was drawn up with the names of those who paid a rent displayed in the appropriate seat place on the plan. Even when seat holders were absent as many of the parish's notabilities often were, no one was allowed to usurp their seats. A number of these seating plans have survived, one for St. Paul's in 1909. They are valuable documents for the social historian.

Already before the opening of St. Paul's, many were advocating the abolition of pew rents and none more eloquently than the lawyer John Coke Fowler who subsequently became stipendiary magistrate at Swansea and vicar's warden at St. Paul's. His book *Church Pews, their Origin and Legal Incidents, with Observations on the Propriety of Abolishing Them* appeared in 1844 and in it he pleaded that the church should become once more the church of the poor. 'Exclusive pews', he wrote, 'tend to expel or keep away the poor. The office of the Church is the cure and salvation of souls, and every consecrated edifice ought to remind us that each soul is entitled to an equal share of her advantages and care. The furniture and arrangements of churches ought to suggest the idea that they are common ground, and that neither the Founder nor the ministers are respecters of persons.' Not everyone shared these views. Many of the pew renters were men who had made their fortunes in industry and commerce, conscious of their rank and importance in society, and unsympathetic to the lower classes. Such a one was John Glasbrook (d.1887), Fowler's successor as vicar's warden. He was a colliery owner and tinplate manufacturer, justice of the peace, successively councillor, alderman and mayor of Swansea. He was against the setting up of a public library in Swansea arguing 'that the working classes have too much knowledge already; it was much easier to manage them twenty years ago; the more education people get, the more difficult they are to manage.' Not all were as class-conscious as Glasbrook. There were those who just liked to sit in a favourite seat and were prepared to pay for it. It was not so much class privilege however but financial expediency which prolonged the continuance of pew rents, for they made a substantial contribution towards the incumbent's stipend, as much as 70 per cent as late at 1904. The stipend at this date was £210 which was made up from fees £16, pew rents £149, special collections £5, and the Vivian endowment £40.

After the Vivian estate was sold in 1919 there was a growing body of opinion in favour of abolition. John Escott, a future churchwarden, remembered how as a young man he was ejected from a reserved seat and became determined to work for the freeing of church seats. Stewart too was very much in favour of putting an end to the practice. When the administrative machinery of the new Church in Wales came fully into operation in the early 1920s the chief *raison d'être* for the retention of pew renting was finally removed, for incumbents now began to be paid a fixed scale of stipends by the Representative Body. In 1925 Stewart decided, not without opposition, to end the practice. Among the representations received by the churchwarden, Mr. Monk, when the news broke, was one from Douglas Campbell Douglas, husband of Violet Averil, eldest daughter of the first Lord Swansea. He expressed the hope that 'the pew will be kept as far as possible for Lady Swansea's use when she is at Sketty Hall. It has always been occupied by the family and has many old associations connected with it and the 1st Lord Swansea. Any books in the pew should be removed and either sent to Sketty Hall or kept in safe custody.' The P.C.C. now proposed that pew rents be abolished 'excepting the Lady Dowager Swansea, the only surviving member at Sketty of the family who founded the church'. In the Easter Vestry of 1926 Stewart was able to announce 'there are now no pew rents in the church, all seats being free'. In 1936 parishioners wished to present Stewart and his wife with a handsome testimonial to mark the completion of twenty-one years' service in the parish. They decided not to accept but persuaded the P.C.C. and parishioners to devote the money collected towards the erection of a new hall and institute at the rear of the school. On 2nd March (the vicar's birthday) the Stewart Hall, as it came to be known, was opened by the Hon. Mrs. Douglas.

Stewart's incumbency was full of incident and achievement but its chief importance for the future history of St. Paul's was its long duration. He was incumbent for twenty-six years, longer than any other with the exception of Bolney. As one reads through the minutes of the P.C.C. during his vicariate one obtains a strong impression of a remarkable rapport developing between the vicar, the church officers and parishioners over the years. After seventeen years as vicar he could tell the Easter Vestry in 1932 that 'it was a joy and pleasure to be vicar of a parish like Sketty'. The members of the P.C.C. were equally appreciative of their vicar. His personality and churchmanship pleased and suited them. The length of his ministry enabled a tradition of a particular type of churchmanship to be established at Sketty. One of Stewart's successors and admirers, Revd. Garfield Hughes James, observed in 1960 that 'vicars of Sketty are fortunate in having in their care a church which has never been a party church and we have all nowadays to be grateful to such men as Stewart for carrying on the good Anglican worship of the middle way'. James

Pugsley, also an admirer of Stewart, rather oddly, viewed him in a different light. By 1928, the year before his death, Pugsley had mellowed since the heady days when he had written his pamphlets, had left the Anglo-Catholic organisation, the English Church Union, and was becoming alarmed at developments at St. Gabriel's. 'I heard the curate there [Vincent Howells] preaching one Sunday evening', wrote Pugsley in a letter to Stewart, 'on purgatory and invocation of saints which was purely Romanist from beginning to end; and on another occasion they recited the Hail Mary, Mother of God . . . on passing the crib in the southern aisle, and for these reasons I dislike the *English Hymnal* . . . .' Pugsley's St. Gabriel's friends were now telling him that he was not a Catholic at all, but only a high churchman of Christ Church type and considered he had changed his views. This Pugsley vigorously denied. 'How Mr. Aubrey's heart would rejoice if he could only see what has since been accomplished at Sketty church which has always been considered High; and you [Stewart] are only reaffirming or developing its old traditions. All honour and success be yours.' Perhaps one of the secrets of Stewart's success was that he appeared all things to all men

In 1941 the bishop invited Stewart to take up the office of Archdeacon of Brecon. Reluctantly he decided to accept and uproot himself from a parish where 'in our great sorrows, in our joys, and in all our undertakings, we have received nothing but kindness and love from all our people'.

Revd. Dr. Joseph Gwyn Davies (1941-46)

Dr. Joseph Gwyn Davies was the most academically qualified and pastorally experienced of all Sketty's incumbents. After taking a 1st in History at Lampeter (1913), he went to Keble College, Oxford graduating with 2nd Class Honours in Theology (1915). He obtained his LL.B. (1921) and LL.D. (1923) from Trinity College, Dublin. He had been ordained deacon in 1915 and priest in 1916 and after serving curacies at Llanelly and Aberystwyth, ministered as vicar at Llanganten (1922-25) and as chaplain of St. Paul's, Valparaiso (1925-28). He then served as vicar successively of Talgarth (1929-35) and St. Andrew's, Cardiff (1935-41). He was examining chaplain to the bishop of Swansea and Brecon, 1931-39 and to the bishop of Llandaff from 1939.

In coming to Sketty he had almost literally leapt from the frying pan into the fire. His parish in Cardiff had been heavily bombed. Damage had been done to the vicarage, school and surrounding streets and the parish hall and scout hall had been destroyed. He now moved to a town which was, with difficulty, recovering from its heaviest period of bombing during the three nights blitz of 19th-21st February 1941. Stewart before handing over the parish to the care of his curate, Revd. H.N. Hancock, had expressed thanks that Sketty had had very few casualties. Evidences of the war and the blitz, however, were everywhere to be seen. The church was blacked out and members of the congregation acted as fire watchers night after night. The Stewart Hall had been taken over by the military and Sketty would soon hear the roar and drone of aircraft from the new fighter station established at Fairwood in May 1941 and the resounding crack of the rocket guns from the new battery set up along Mumbles Rd. And the air raids continued. On one night the church was ringed with incendiary bombs and in a raid on 16th February 1943 Sketty Green and Vivian Rd. suffered badly. It was fortunate that Stewart had arranged for the removal of the stained glass before his departure.

Although Davies had received his theological training at the Anglo-Catholic Keble College – a College which, it has been estimated, supplied more converts to Rome in its first thirty years 'than seven other Colleges in twice the time', he conducted the services in the traditional manner with additional services of intercession for those on active service and special parade services for the military and welfare organisations. Almost all the services were well attended. There was a very large Sunday School managed by twenty-five teachers and a successful kindergarten supervised by Mrs. Jones.

In 1942 the vicar began to point to the future. The church, he said, should set its mind on two things: propaganda (a favourite wartime word by which he meant evangelization and mission) and church extension. He was very conscious of the supreme sacrifice being made by so many in what was increasingly perceived as a just war and was already planning the building of a daughter church, to be dedicated, as their lasting memorial, to All Souls. One hundred and one Sketty people were eventually killed in the conflict. In 1946 the P.C.C. was pleased to report that the local builders Bennett Bros. had replaced the stained glass windows very efficiently and at a very reasonable cost. The bells were put in order and when they first rang out the vicar gave the Hon. Mrs. Douglas, then in Scotland, an opportunity to hear them by holding the telephone receiver outside the vicarage window. In his last P.C.C. meeting tribute was paid to his most inspiring sermons and the magnificent letters he wrote for the parish magazine. Dr. Davies left Sketty in October 1946 to become dean of Monmouth. He died in 1952 and was buried in the cathedral close at St. David's. A wooden cross over the pulpit at St. Paul's commemorates his ministry.

Dissension and Division: An Anglo-Catholic Interlude: Revd. John Cyril Hill (1946-50)

The Revd. John Cyril Hill was instituted vicar of St. Paul's by Bishop E.W. Williamson and inducted by the Ven. Harold Stepney Williams on 20th November 1946. An Exhibitioner at Jesus College, Oxford, he had had a distinguished academic career, taking a 2nd Class in Classics Moderations in 1926 and graduating with 1st Class Honours in Theology in 1928. He was ordained deacon in 1928 and priest in 1929 and served as curate at Tenby before becoming a chaplain at Brecon cathedral and curate of St. Mary's Brecon, 1939-40. During the war he was a Forces Chaplain and served during the gruelling Italian campaigns. Before coming to Sketty he held a brief post-war curacy at St. Barnabas, Carlisle. Archdeacon Williams, who had chaired the Diocesan Patronage Board which appointed him, is said to have confided privately that he had secured the right man for Sketty but had disclaimed this later when the troubles began. To understand the dissension which followed one needs to be aware of the disposition of church parties in Swansea and district at this time.

Revd. J. C. Hill
(St. Paul's Church Archives/ West Glamorgan Record Office)

The level of churchmanship in the majority of churches within the archdeaconry of Gower in the years approaching mid-century could be described as broad to low. The Anglo-Catholic movement within the Church of England and the Church in Wales, although it had reached the zenith of its influence during the 1930s and 1940s, had taken neither widespread nor deep root within the archdeaconry. Nevertheless, there were a number of churches which were conspicuous for varying degrees of high churchmanship. Christ Church, founded in 1872 as a daughter church of St. Mary's, acquired its own parish in 1874 and during the vicariate of Revd. Eli Clarke (1874-96) developed a relatively high level of churchmanship based on Tractarian teaching. Clarke, originally an evangelical, had come under the influence of his warden Charles Bath, a well-to-do ship owner and copper merchant, a fearless advocate of Catholic principles and chairman of the local branch of the English Church

Union, one of the chief mouthpieces of the Anglo-Catholic cause. This tradition of churchmanship was maintained by subsequent incumbents.

At St. Gabriel's, founded in 1889, the movement towards Anglo-Catholicism was swift. When Hussey Vivian laid the foundation stone he confidently hoped 'that nothing but sound Protestant Christianity would be heard within its walls'. Its second vicar, Revd. John Pollock (1891-1911), however, became increasingly sympathetic to the Catholic movement and by the 1920s St. Gabriel's had become a full-blown Anglo-Catholic church, the flagship of the movement in Swansea. William Llewelyn Morgan (1846-1927), the founder of the church and the vicar's warden, was sensitive to the feelings of low church parishioners who came to 11 a.m. Matins and had a fan installed in the chancel roof to clear the air of incense before they arrived. It is still there.

All Saints, Oystermouth had developed a high church tradition under the Revd. Harold Stepney Williams, vicar between 1898 and 1938, and Archdeacon of Gower when Hill was appointed. He was a Prayer Book Catholic, an adherent of the branch theory that the Anglican communion was one of the three branches of the One, Holy, Catholic and Apostolic Church. He considered the Eucharist to be 'the highest, greatest and best service of the Church Militant here on earth'. He had introduced vestments in the 1920s and in the mid-1930s, at the suggestion of his curate Revd. T. Illtyd Jenkins, had allowed incense to be used at the christening of his first grandchild. He was to play a key role in the troubles of John Hill's incumbency.

At St. Paul's, Landore, consecrated in 1903, a moderately high level of churchmanship had developed during the vicariate of Revd. W.D.G. Wilkinson (1935-39). But his successor and friend, Revd. Archibald Samuel and his curate Revd. K.J. Gillingham, created at Landore, to use the words of one of its curates at this time (Revd. Ian Burton, later the Orthodox monk Archimandrite Barnabas), 'an advanced stronghold of Anglo-papal Catholicism . . . not without much opposition, and even censure from parishioners and church authorities'. Landore was, he writes, 'the most advanced parish in Wales and possibly not surpassed in any parish in any place in the Anglican Communion'. Fr. Samuel was a friend of John Hill and Fr. Gillingham a former parishioner of St. Paul's, Sketty.

Such were the churches which became points of reference in the controversy which now began. Trouble surfaced officially in a meeting of the Finance Committee and Parochial Church Council held on 31st December 1946. A letter from Mr. W. Lewis was read in which he protested against the Anglo-Catholic practices of the vicar. These, he declared 'were not in the best interests of our church' and had caused concern and apprehension among many parishioners. The vicar replied that he was not aware that any unauthorised changes had been made but that all was in keeping with the Prayer Book. He admitted he was an Anglo-Catholic and declared that he wished to make Holy Communion the focal point of worship. Many more voiced their disapproval of changes already made and hoped that the vicar would return to the former simple worship which had been the hall-mark of Christian life within the parish. Another group within the P.C.C. supported the vicar, said that they had the utmost faith in his mission and thought the changes had been misinterpreted. Once they had been explained and understood, they argued, they would be more readily accepted.

Discord continued in the P.C.C. held on 25th March 1947 in which the vicar declared that he had no intention of departing from the changes he had made. Mr. J.E. Pratt's motion that a deputation be made to the bishop to bring to his notice the feelings of parishioners was carried with fourteen voting in favour, seven against and one abstaining. The deputation was to be composed of Messrs. James Isaac, J.E. Pratt and John Escott (soon to be People's Warden).

At the Easter Vestry held on 16th April 1947 there were one hundred and fifty parishioners present but the deputation had not yet met the bishop. The meeting proceeded peaceably enough. The vicar admitted there had been difficulties but hoped that these would now be overcome and that all would go forward with the united resolve of working together for the good of the parish and the greater glory of God. The deputation met the bishop a week later on 22nd April. Bishop Williamson, a quiet, scholarly man, already wearied by similar troubles at Landore, invited them to sit around a table for a friendly discussion. He himself, he admitted, made his confession and thought that the vicar had kept the promises he had made. There were, he said, a number of sins, among them Pride, Arrogance and Self-righteousness, each one of which was enough to take a soul to hell. He hoped there would be an improvement in the prevailing conditions, but if not, they could come back and see him again.

The content of these discussions were reported by Mr. Isaac to the P.C.C. held on 29th July 1947 at which Archdeacon H.S. Williams was present. This was a crucial meeting. All the main grievances against the vicar were aired and the vicar given an opportunity to reply. The first grievance was that the vicar had uprooted the Children's Chapel within a few weeks of his arrival and removed the small chairs and books to the back of the church. Again the practice of Confession was taught; here the Archdeacon interposed to say that he was quite satisfied with Confession 'as far as the Prayer Book guided them on the subject'. Mr. Escott continued and said that the vicar did not stick to the form of service in the Book of Common Prayer and that the Communion service was the most debased form of service ever held. The wafer was not put into their hands as was customary.

The vicar replied that he was surprised to find three altars in the church and had used all three for celebrations of Holy Communion. He would in future confine celebrations to the other two altars. Mr. E. Bennett said that the former curate, Mr. Hancock, had instituted the children's service in their chapel but that attendances had dropped after his departure. It was not right to blame the vicar for what had happened before he came to Sketty. The vicar had not interfered in his administration of the Sunday Schools. He ascribed a lot of the trouble to a lack of co-operation from the church officials and far too much attention was paid to tittle-tattle. The vicar, in reply to the claim that certain prayers not in the Prayer Book were used during the Communion service, claimed a right to his private prayers and if these led to long silences he expected the congregation would then be engaged in their own devotions. This was not entirely true. The vicar, before and after the Consecration, was using the more elaborate prayers to be found in the *English Missal*. This was a translation of the Roman Missal, first published in 1933 to mark the centenary of the Oxford Movement and used by advanced Anglo-Catholics. Another parishioner was distressed to hear the vicar speaking of introducing acolytes and incense and that less importance was now paid to Matins and Evensong. The changes could at least have been discussed with the people. The vicar replied that he had indeed arranged a series of Lenten lectures to explain various matters but few of the parochial church councillors had attended. Mr. Glyn Davies said that the church was split into two camps with churches like St. Barnabas, St. Jude's and Manselton on the one side and Christ Church, Landore and St. Gabriel's on the other.

The Archdeacon tried to reassure the meeting that Sketty was not going the way of Landore; if it was, he would be the first to go against the vicar. He had faith in the vicar but if the time came when his conscience told him he should not stay, he was quite certain the vicar would go. There had, he said, been little teaching in church matters generally, and little in Sketty. He himself was a thorough Catholic, 'not Roman of course, but Catholic and Protestant'. He liked ritual, good music and vestments and referred the P.C.C. to the Prayer Book rubric regarding the rightness of vestments. He had, as a young priest, wanted to introduce vestments but found it necessary to exercise patience and tact before the congregation would accept the idea. They should not be used unless the mass of the people was behind the vicar. The vicar, meanwhile, should be patient and discreet and show less stubbornness. He emphasised that Matins and Evensong were not obligatory but that the Eucharist was and urged parishioners to pull together and make Sketty a real 'church' church.

Crucial though the meeting was in bringing grievances into the open and anxious though the Archdeacon was to achieve a reconciliation by being scrupulously fair, the meeting achieved nothing. The dispute rumbled on from one P.C.C. meeting to another, each becoming more acrimonious and obstructive. The conflict poisoned parish life and stifled initiatives in other fields. Nothing was done at this period to forward the establishment of the long-awaited church at Tycoch. Essentially the dispute was between two irreconcilable parties. On the one hand was an 'old guard' of church officers, allied to a substantial body of parishioners, most probably representing the majority of the parish. They were at ease and comfortable with the regime of services established in the long and fondly-remembered vicariate of Stewart in which Matins and Evensong held hallowed positions, and did not wish to see this regime disturbed or overthrown. They were low and broad church and were equally unwilling to have any truck with Anglo-Catholic practices which many considered would lead inevitably to the extremism of Landore.

On the other hand was the vicar, an avowed Anglo-Catholic who wished to give priority to the Eucharist with appropriate accompanying ceremonial, at the expense of Matins and Evensong. He had an additional agenda: to supplement the use of the Book of Common Prayer with that of the *English Missal*, to introduce the practice of Confession and Catholic devotions, such as the rosary and devotions to the Blessed Sacrament. Supporting the vicar was a strong but not particularly vocal minority following. It included some members of youth organisations and especially Cymry'r Groes (Welsh People of the Cross), who were not able to vote in the P.C.C. Interestingly, there was a marked increase in the number and frequency of communions during this vicariate and more vocations to the priesthood were fostered than at any other period in the history of St. Paul's. But it was perhaps the Revd. H.N. Hancock, the curate, who sowed most of the seeds of these vocations and the Revd. Harry Craven Williams, a priest with a remarkable gift for leadership, who later nurtured them to fruition. The dispute was exacerbated by a clash of personalities; the main protagonists on each side were stubborn and unwilling to compromise. John Hill, though a devout and sincere priest, did not have sufficient pastoral experience to have his views generally accepted. Even sympathisers would perhaps admit that changes were introduced too swiftly without sufficient preparation or consultation.

In 1949 bigger guns were brought to bear on the vicar. In the P.C.C. meeting of 1st February Judge Rowe Harding, soon to be appointed Chancellor of the Diocese of St. David's, asked the vicar to give some assurance that he would moderate his actions, give up any practice contrary to the wishes of the majority and respect low church opinion. At the P.C.C. of 31st January 1950 resolutions calling for the withdrawal, removal and resignation of the vicar were passed with eighteen voting for and two against. In May 1950 the bishop and archdeacon met the vicar and formally received his resignation.

The Revd. John Hill moved to Caverswall and after serving curacies there and at Great Bookham (1950-56), withdrew from the ministry and took a teaching post at Hamilton House School in Ealing. He became a Roman Catholic and refused to draw the clerical pension that was his due.

CHAPTER 3

'Church and Kingdom in an Age of Change and Doubt', 1950-99

Hymns Ancient & Modern, New Standard Ed., No. 464

BACKGROUND

After 1950 the Church had to face an unprecedented period of social, cultural and economic change. The establishment of the welfare state and the years of post-war austerity were followed by a period of full employment and relative affluence – 'you've never had it so good', declared Harold Macmillan. Yet the affluence heralded in an era which boded ill for the Church. At first, in the 1950s and early1960s, the churches had only to contend with the opening of cinemas and pubs on a Sunday and on Good Friday, the most sensitive day in the Christian year. Bishop Glyn Simon (1954-57) initiated a number of processions of witness in which the parishioners of St. Paul's played a full part. But in fact the influence of the cinema was beginning to wane and it was television and the increase in car ownership which was eventually to transform the way people were to spend their time outside working hours. Favourite television shows, lunch at popular restaurants and car trips to places of local interest began making inroads on the numbers attending Sunday School and threatened to phase out Evensong as a popular, well-attended service. Television programmes like *Ready, Steady, Go* and *Six Five Special* started to generate a new pop culture which was to take many of the young from the Church despite frantic attempts to create and maintain church-sponsored youth clubs. Much of the early pop scene was innocent enough but the lyrics of the Rock generation that followed had a more sinister ring which chimed well with the 'permissive age' and the so-called 'new morality' (really the old immorality) of the 1960s and 1970s. The purple hearts of the Mods and Rockers of the 1950s were now giving way to heroin and other hard drugs in the big cities and by the late 1970s the middle class areas of Swansea West and the housing estates of Swansea's old industrial heartland in the east were being infected. Both areas were now suffering in varying degrees from a new wave of unemployment. The introduction of the pill, the legalisation of abortion and the liberalisation of the divorce laws were placing added pressures on the traditional family. The new alternative culture was largely indifferent to the life and mission of the Church and reinforced the already powerfully-flowing tide of secularism.

Leaders of the Anglican communion have always been conscious of the Church's social responsibilities and have spoken up for the disadvantaged, sometimes to the annoyance of ultra-conservative politicians – witness the reception of Archbishop Runcie's report *Faith in the City* (1985). There were troubles and issues enough to respond to in Britain, particularly after the conflict in Northern Ireland was resumed. The killing of the first British soldier in 1970 was followed by 'Bloody Sunday' in 1972 and the resumption of I.R.A. terrorism. But in the 1970s and 1980s Britain had become part of the global village. The ends of the earth were now only a day's journey away, global communication had become instantaneous and continuous and images of famine, distress and slaughter, often in the decolonised areas of Africa, were nightly being flashed on television screens. Each postal delivery seemed to contain appeals from a variety of charities, producing feelings of helplessness and compassion fatigue among those who received them. The Church was inevitably drawn into the work of Christian aid and it has reflected well on St. Paul's parish that individuals have been prepared, with members of other churches, to travel out to Romania, Bosnia and Kosovo with medical supplies, food and clothing.

The Christian Church as an institution also went through a period of revolutionary change during this period, partly in response to social change, partly in pursuance of earlier initiatives. The Roman Church under Pius XII had already in the 1950s made rather unexpected moves in introducing evening communion and relaxing the eucharistic fast, much to the bewilderment of the Anglo-Catholic wing of the Anglican communion. But the calling of the Vatican Council by Pope John XXIII (1958-63) was as unexpected as it was momentous in its consequences. As the Council proceeded and as its programme began to be implemented after its closure, it almost seemed that the Roman Church was moving in a Protestant direction, remedying some of the grievances that had produced the Protestant Reformation. The Council certainly gave an encouraging fillip to the liturgical movement which was already under way in both the Roman and Anglican Churches. The Alternative Service Books of the Church of England, and the Blue Book (1967) and the revised Green Books (1984) of the Church in Wales, in spite of the imperfections pointed out by critics, were notable achievements. The Green Books had taken on board much of the message and teaching of the Oxford Movement. 'Indeed', wrote Richard

Hart, curate of St. Paul's, Sketty, writing in the *Beacon* (March 1987) 'all the alterations from Cranmer's service to our present Green Books have been in a Catholic direction and also much influenced by the past'.

The Vatican Council and the Decree on Ecumenism (1964) in particular gave added stimulus to an already burgeoning ecumenical movement. Under the general umbrella of the British Council of Churches, a number of local councils were formed in the 1970s and 1980s, among them the Swansea Council of Churches and the Sketty Council of Churches. The latter had a particularly fruitful and vigorous life and after the launch of CYTUN became Cytun in Sketty or Churches Together in Sketty. With the ecumenical movement flourishing nationally in England and Wales, could there be a theological convergence of the Roman and Anglican communions? In 1960 before the Vatican Council had been summoned, Archbishop Fisher who was always regarded as, to use Professor Adrian Hasting's phrase, 'intuitively suspicious of Rome', visited the Pope on his (Fisher's) way home from the Holy Land. Pope John met him in his study and read out a statement, specially prepared for him by the Curia, which referred in traditional manner to 'the return of our separated brethren to the Mother Church'. Fisher, in characteristically schoolmasterly fashion, interrupted; 'Your Holiness, not *return*'. The Pope, puzzled, asked, 'Not return? Why not?' 'None of us can go backwards', Fisher replied 'We are each now running on parallel courses; we are looking forward, until, in God's own time, our two courses approximate and meet.' The Pope paused and said 'You are right'. After the Vatican Council during the pontificate of Paul VI, who was on friendly terms with a number of Anglican bishops and referred to the Anglican Communion as 'our sister church', the hopes that the parallel lines would converge were real enough and many looked forward to some form of union in a not too distant future. The future was to bring many disappointments as well as some solid achievements, as we shall see.

Overshadowing all these activities were the changing fortunes, the peaks and troughs of the Cold War, in which East and West confronted each other for over half a century. Britain, with its huge stock pile of atomic weapons in Berkshire and East Anglia, acted as America's forward base in the event of nuclear war and was at the vulnerable centre of it. In retrospect it is chilling to realise how close the world was to the edge of annihilation during the Cuban missile crisis (1962). There were other, less serious periods of tension, waiting to escalate into crisis, and it was not until after the era of Gorbachev and the break-up of the Soviet empire that President Bush was able to celebrate the end of the Cold War in his State of the Union speech of 1991.

Revd. Harry Craven Williams, 1950-58

Ven. H. C. Williams
(St. Paul's Church Archives/ West Glamorgan Record Office)

The Revd. Harry Craven Williams was appointed to bring peace to a deeply-riven parish after the departure of the Revd. John Hill. A native of Manselton, he was educated at Dynevor School and University College, Swansea where he graduated in Philosophy in 1932. In his college days he had been a good athlete; he had run for Wales as an even-timer in the 100 yards and had taken a notable part in the social and administrative life of the student body. He was ordained deacon in 1933 and priest in 1934. After ministerial training at St. Michael's College, Llandaff, he served his first and only curacy at St. Mary's, Swansea before becoming an army chaplain, 1939-46. On demobilization he was appointed vicar of St. Jude's, 1946-50. Immediately before his institution and induction at St. Paul's, the first words the Archdeacon of Gower greeted him with were 'Don't forget, one of your first jobs is to build a new daughter church'. He had scarcely moved into the vicarage when he was also informed that the church would in a few months be celebrating its centenary and that he would have to produce a booklet on its history, arrange for a play to be written for the Dramatic Society and see that the bells were put in order so that they would ring out for the centenary celebrations. He tackled all these tasks with characteristic energy and determination. The money for the restoration of the bells, amounting to about £1,000, was collected within weeks and the work put in hand. With the help of previous incumbents still living, together with Gwen John and Canon D. Ambrose Jones, he produced a well-illustrated and valuable history, *The Story of St. Paul's Church, Sketty, 1850-1950.* Miss Isabel Westcott, a lecturer in the English Department of the University College and a great churchwoman whose Christian work within and outside the parish covered many decades, wrote the play. Enough money was collected, too, for a contribution to be made to the rebuilding fund of the blitzed church of St. Mary, Swansea. The planning and funding of All Souls Church took much longer and this work and the additions to the fabric of St. Paul's, made during his incumbency, are chronicled in greater detail in Chapter Five.

He was a conscientious parish priest and ran the parish on traditional lines, restoring the type of worship to which Sketty had become accustomed during the incumbency of H.J. Stewart. Through his acquaintance with the sporting, business and administrative leaders of the town and the university and attendance at their functions he was able to give St. Paul's and the work of the church generally a high profile in the town. He was a popular preacher; his sermons were well-prepared, forcefully presented and delivered without notes. He preached to packed congregations at Sunday evensong. Acting on an idea first sown by his friend and successor Garfield James he arranged for the College Extra-Mural Department to run refresher courses in theology for ministers and lay people of all denominations. They were highly appreciated. He was made a canon of Brecon Cathedral before being appointed vicar of St. Mary's, Swansea in 1958.

REVD. GARFIELD HUGHES JAMES, 1958-79

The career of the Revd. Garfield James had, up to a point, run on parallel lines to that of his predecessor. He too was a product of Manselton where two generations of his forebears had lived. He had been educated at Dynevor School, Swansea and Swansea University College, where he took a 2nd in Philosophy and graduated in 1934. His ministerial training was spent at St. Michael's College, Llandaff. Ordained deacon in 1935 and priest in 1936, he served a curacy at St. Mary's (1935-40) before becoming an army chaplain during World War II. On his return he held a curacy at St. Jude's (1946-47). There the parallel career ends. He served as a chaplain at Butlin's, Pwllheli from 1947 to1948, Bishop's Messenger (Swansea and Brecon) from 1948 to 1951 and vicar of Manselton, 1951-58. He was an admirer of the Revd. H.J. Stewart and, as has been noted, a close friend of the Revd. Harry Craven Williams whose tribute he wrote for the Diocesan Leaflet (October 1979) when the latter retired as Archdeacon of Gower.

Garfield James was, like his predecessor Stewart, an advocate of 'good Anglican worship of the middle way' and his incumbency, the third longest in the history of St. Paul's, tended to strengthen and confirm the tradition of worship established by Stewart with the danger perhaps of it becoming ossified, making it less open to experiment and change. Warm, sociable, sincere and kind, he endeared himself to his parishioners but he could be infuriatingly forgetful and stories are still told of his being called away from mowing the lawn to officiate at weddings or funerals he had forgotten. He once said that he never reached the dizzy heights of an

St. Paul's Choir in 1962
(B. Walker)

archdeaconry but he was in fact appointed Chancellor of the diocese in 1971, ranking as senior member of the chapter after the Dean. He became Rural Dean of Clyne in 1978. During his incumbency St. Paul's first purchased houses for its assistant clergy. He fostered the growth and consolidation of All Souls which had been opened in 1957 and gave a free hand to his assistant clergy who manned it before it became a separate parish in 1972. He also planned and saw the establishment of Holy Trinity, Sketty Park in 1969. These activities and his improvements to the fabric are dealt with in a later chapter.

On Sunday 24th January 1965 at 11 a.m. a service was held in thanks-giving for the restored beauty of the church. In the previous year the interior of the church had been completely redecorated. At the service an aumbry for the reservation of the Blessed Sacrament in the Vivian Chapel was dedicated by the Archdeacon. The aumbry had been given in memory of Edmund Bennett, captain of the sidesmen of the church, and to com-memorate his long service to the Sunday School. He had been, as we have seen, a loyal supporter of the Revd. John Hill. The question of reserva-tion had troubled the Anglican Communion since the 1920s. 'More than any other issue', writes Professor Adrian Hastings, 'it came near to tear-ing the Church of England apart'. To reserve the sacrament for commu-nicating the sick was reasonable enough in a busy parish, particularly when it had responsibilities to hospital patients, as St. Paul's had over the years to Cefn Coed Mental Hospital (opened 1932) and later to Singleton Hospital (opened 1967). The only alternative to reservation was for the vicar to celebrate a brief but complete eucharist each time a sick person required communion. Once reservation is admitted, however, it presupposes the continuing sacramental presence of Christ. The prayers used by the Archdeacon and printed in the service leaflet, made this very clear. Such a presence could become a focus for devotion by the Catholic-minded, a practice anathema to low churchmen.

The vicar was very conscious of the dilemma and sensitive to the feelings of his low church parishioners. Just before Christmas in 1966 he received from the publishers a batch of church diaries which were to go on sale to parishioners. He quickly warned them in the parish magazine that they contained 'some matter that is not according to the taste of many of you, nor does it suit my taste. I see no harm in calling the Holy Communion service 'the Mass', but it is not in our tradition to do so. And in any case the words 'Communion' and 'Eucharist' are far more meaningful'.

Yet no one was a greater enemy of sectarianism nor a more committed worker for the ideals of the ecumenical movement than Garfield James. Relations between St. Paul's and the Free Churches in the Sketty area had always tended to be good, perhaps because of its style of churchmanship. But friendly ties with the Roman Church did not exist. The official Roman line until Vatican II was that Catholic participation in non-Catholic assemblies would confirm the erroneous view that one religion was as good as another. Indeed, at a Convocation held at Canterbury held in 1955, Archbishop Fisher denounced the Roman Catholic Church as 'perhaps the greatest hindrance to the advancement of the Kingdom of God among men' because of its practice of ecclesiastical apartheid. The pontificate of Pope John (1959-63), the second Vatican Council, the Decree on Ecumenism (1964), Archbishop Michael Ramsey's visit to Rome in 1966, the Anglican-Roman Catholic International Commission (ARCIC) set up in 1969 and the ecumenical activities of the World Council of Churches and related organisations changed the atmosphere irrevocably. 'Nothing has given me more pleasure this Christmas (1964)', wrote Garfield James in the parish magazine, 'than receiving a card from Canon O'Keiffe' (the priest in charge of St. Benedict's Roman Catholic Church). During the second half of the 1960s and during the 1970s there developed a remarkable degree of Christian fellowship among the churches of Swansea based on the Lund principle (1952): 'Should not our Churches ask themselves . . . whether they should not act together in all matters, except those in which deep differences of conviction compel them to act separately.' The activities which promoted this sense of fellowship – joint worship, talks, retreats, prayer and house study groups – took place partly under the organizational umbrella of the Swansea Council of Churches but were initiated too by committed activists who, while taking a full part in the Council's activities, supplemented its work. Among the Free Churches, the Revd. Noel Davies, a Congregational minister, and the Revd. George Hughes, a Baptist minister, took notable parts. The former was secretary of the Council of Churches for Wales and President of the Swansea Council of Churches. At St. Paul's, apart from the vicar who rarely missed an ecumenical event, his curate the Revd. Robert M. Paterson (Holy Trinity, 1973-8) acted as secretary for the Swansea Council of Churches in the late 1970s and did much to warn parents of the dangers of their children having dealings with the Unification Church, the 'Moonies', who were recruiting in the Swansea area at this time. Miss Joyce Phillips deserves special mention here. She was a council member of the International Ecumenical Fellowship, the St. Paul's representative on the Sketty Council of Churches, and the forger of the first church link between Swansea and Mannheim in 1975. Her tireless work for the ecumenical cause has spanned four incumbencies. It was Ron Howells who provided the link with the Roman Church. Although a Sketty man, he was a parishioner of St. David's Roman Catholic Church where Father John Grumbaldeston had made a special study of the *Decree of Ecumenism* and instructed his parishioners in its teaching. Ron Howells played a major role in the ecumenical movement for over two decades becoming President of the Swansea Council of Churches in 1977. He gave talks, preached and organised quiet days and prayer groups and was well-known to Sketty folk. At one period in the late 1960s one could have observed four Roman Catholics, Ron Howells among them, at Coleg Coffa, Swansea Memorial College, sitting at the feet of Professor Trefor Evans learning Hebrew and hearing him talk on the Law, the Prophets and the Scriptures. Ron Howell's book, *A Tale of Two Grandmothers: Memoirs of an Ecumenist, 1965-85* (1994) chronicles the achievements of these years and conveys too the excitement and exhilaration of the movement's leaders in a period when they held high hopes for the union of the Christian churches in a foreseeable future. Even so, there were early disappointments. Garfield James, although he had reservations, was disappointed that the Anglican-Methodist scheme of unity had failed at the end of the 1960s.

Garfield James was a well-read cleric and he would sometimes go into the pulpit carrying a pile of books which he would consult and read from in the course of his sermons. His wide reading was also displayed in his letters to the parish magazine which he used not only to inform, instruct and edify but also to air his opinions on a whole range of topics. He was scathing in his criticism of the twelve-storey Telephone Exchange (1970) in the Strand and of what the planners had done to Swansea. He particularly enjoyed reading Colin Rosser and Christopher Harris's book *The*

Revd. G. H. James
(M. M. James)

Family and Social Change (1965). He drew from it and added material of his own to produce an entertaining thumb-nail sketch of the sociology of Sketty. The real growth of Sketty, he wrote, occurred after World War I when the number of people in Sketty doubled and the number of houses trebled. Between 1951 and 1961 the population remained numerically almost static. Since 1961 when the Sketty population was estimated at 11,300 there had been another period of rapid expansion. Regarding social class distribution, he continued, 'Sketty is known as a middle class area (indeed the very name is said to carry with it in some minds over-tones of social superiority) but in fact, with one exception, there is no part of Swansea so equally divided in its social structure'. More Welsh was spoken in the area than one might think for 21% of the population speak Welsh either fluently or partly. Of six selected localities only Morriston and Landore have a larger number of fluent Welsh speakers. Although its population is as large as Morriston, Sketty has only two public houses to Morriston's twenty one. It also, he continued, has the largest Bingo hall in Swansea with 18,000 members, of whom 1,500 to 2,000 arrive every night by bus or car. He added, with feigned hauteur, 'few of the residents of Sketty appear to belong'.

Chancellor Garfield James left Sketty in April 1979 and took up a post at St. Mary's, Weybridge, Surrey. He returned to St. Paul's on 27th December 1986 to celebrate the Holy Eucharist in thanksgiving for his having served fifty years as a priest and retired, with his wife Marjorie, initially to Llangennith where he assisted the Revd. Robert Williams when he was Rector of Reynoldston, and latterly at Harford Court, Sketty. He died on 11th April 1990 at Weybridge Hospital.

Canon Ilar Roy Luther Thomas, 1979-89

Canon Ilar Roy Luther Thomas was inducted and instituted vicar on 31st July 1979. A native of Llansamlet, he was educated at St. David's College, Lampeter where he graduated in 1951 and at St. Michael's College, Llandaff. He was ordained deacon in 1953 and priest in 1954. He came to Sketty with extensive pastoral and administrative experience. After serving curacies at Oystermouth and Gorseinon, he was rector of Llanbadarn Fawr with Llandegley, 1959, and with Llanfihangel Rhydithon, 1960-65 and vicar of Knighton, 1966-79 and had been made Canon of Brecon Cathedral in 1975. Before his appointment to Sketty he had already agreed to take on the irksome and exacting task of editing the diocesan directory but there were now more pressing pastoral problems to face. Mr. John M. Davies, the organist, reported a severe decline in the number of choristers; the Revd. Martin Reed, the curate, was concerned that the Sunday Schools were declining. 'It's not for a shortage of available children, or for lack of hard work by the teachers we have', he wrote in the parish magazine, 'but due to a total lack of interest by much of the rest of the church'. Pleas for extra teachers had not received a response. Mr. Gordon Jones was equally concerned with this problem and a lively debate ensued in the pages of the magazine and in church meetings. Membership numbers, as revealed by the electoral roll (admittedly never an infallible guide to real numbers), also appeared to be falling. Sketty was not alone in experiencing difficulty in attracting and retaining the young and in recruiting new members. A 1982 *Census of the Churches in Wales* had revealed a dramatic decline in churchgoing. An acknowledgement by church officers that St. Paul's had problems common to many other churches did not beget complacency. The Scout troop was reformed in January 1980 after a period of temporary abeyance. An attempt was made to breath new life into the Sunday Schools and youth groups by giving them a new image through a change of names (Pathfinders, Pioneers, Agape and Cogs). A new society for young women was formed, *Women on Wednesday* with a more open membership and supplementing the work of the Mothers' Union and Lady's Guild. A branch of Cymry'r Groes, a national youth organization first established in 1944, was revived in the parish in 1986. Working groups such as Outreach and Worship were established to feed back information to the P.C.C. for action.

The vicar was anxious, too, to bind the two communities of St. Paul's and its daughter church Holy Trinity closer together. Under normal circumstances it would have been natural for a daughter church like Holy Trinity to develop its own life and eventually acquire separate parochial status. In a time when vocations to the priesthood were falling and the supply of clergy was drying up through retirement and death, this was no longer feasible. Early in 1981 the first congregational meeting of the whole parish was held and in 1984, as a result of a Parish Life Conference, the P.C.C. unanimously decided to arrange, for an experimental period, a joint parish eucharist for the two churches to be held on the first Sunday in the month at 10 a.m. to replace the 8 a.m. and 11 a.m. services at the parish church and the 9.30 a.m. service at Holy Trinity. A vote in 1985 revealed that 57% were in favour of the new arrangement and 43% against. A two thirds majority was really needed and after a further period of trial the experiment was abandoned in October 1985.

What most taxed the energies of the vicar, church officers and parishioners at this time, however, were fabric problems at the parish church and its associated buildings at Stewart Hall. The response of the parish to these problems is chronicled in the chapter on the fabric.

Ecumenical enthusiasm had perhaps reached its peak in the immediate aftermath of Pope John Paul's visit to Britain in 1982. The following year saw the establishment of the Sketty Council of Churches (later to be replaced by CYTUN: Churches Together in Sketty in the early 1990s) with Miss Joyce Phillips as St. Paul's representative. But in spite of the frequently-arranged days of ecumenical worship and study which included those sponsored by the new movement Covenanting for Unity, ecumenical fervour began to cool. 'It is the faithful few', reported the vicar in 1986, 'who have joined the ecumenical study groups and attended the services during Lent. The opportunities are there for all of us right here in the parish, but do we take them?' At about the same time Archbishop Ward of Cardiff in his address to the Governing Body of the Church in Wales referred to the quest for unity as a '*via dolorosa* which would require a total dependence on the gifts of the Holy Spirit, and an obedience by all Christians to God's will. The Risen Lord will . . . show us what we must leave behind in the empty tomb of yesterday's divisions'.

In 1987 Canon Luther Thomas was appointed Chancellor of the diocese and in 1989 he retired from Sketty to become Archdeacon of Gower.

Revd. Stephen Brooks, 1990-93

The new vicar was a native of Llansamlet. He was educated at Trinity College, Carmarthen and University of Wales, Aberystwyth where he graduated B.Ed. in 1976. He went on to St. Stephen's House, Oxford for his ministerial training and graduated B.A. in Theology in 1978. He was ordained deacon in 1979 and priest in 1980. He served a curacy at All Saints, Oystermouth between 1979-81 and was a minor canon of Brecon Cathedral and curate of St. Mary's, Brecon between 1981-84. While at Brecon he was Diocesan Youth Chaplain, Bishop's Visitor for Schools, Director of the Religious Education Resource Centre and Warden of Ordinands. He was vicar of St. Paul's, Landore from 1984 until his appointment as vicar of Sketty in 1990.

His vicariate began with great promise. The new parish centre was built from money realised from the sale of Stewart Hall and opened in 1992. He introduced eucharistic vestments, the adoption of which had long been resisted, though they had been in use in most Swansea churches for some time and had been introduced in All Souls when it was still a daughter church of St. Paul's. He had settled well into the parish, preached to substantial congregations and was extremely popular. He had just been appointed canon of Brecon Cathedral when a scandal involving sexual offences broke in the press which brought trauma and tragedy to so many people and forced his resignation. The former incumbent, now Archdeacon Luther Thomas, stepped in to administer the parish until a new incumbent was appointed. He was ably assisted by the Revd. Rebecca Swyer and Revd. Graham Noyce, the parish's assistant clergy, who constantly traversed the parish at this time to bring counsel and comfort to parishioners.

Revd. Robert John Williams, 1994-99

The bishop invited the Revd. Robert Williams to take over the parish early in 1994 and his induction and institution took place on 22nd June 1994. The bell ringers rang a special ¼ peel to welcome him to the parish. A native of Brynhyfryd, he had been educated at Cartrefle College of Education, Wrexham and University College, Bangor, graduating B.Ed. in 1974 and obtaining his M.A. in 1992. He was ordained deacon in 1976 and priest in 1977. In the following decade he became well-known in the Swansea area, for he served as curate of St. Mary's, Swansea under Revd. Don Lewis (1976-8) and Anglican chaplain at University College, Swansea (1984-88). He moved to St. Asaph diocese in 1988 to become rector of Denbigh and Nantglyn and remained there until appointed to

Sketty. He was appointed a canon of Brecon Cathedral in 1995. During his early clerical career he held a variety of administrative posts which prepared him well for life in a busy, populous parish.

His first priorities were to bring peace and healing to a parish still in deep shock and to restore trust in the clergy and the church. These tasks took time but were performed with care, sensitivity and compassion. It was now that the decision to sell the Stewart Hall was convincingly demonstrated to have been a wise one. The vicar with the assistance of Sue Knight and the Management Committee transformed the newly-built parish centre into the hub of parochial administration, giving backing to the many church-sponsored recreational societies which met there and special support to those specialist church societies which promoted the pastoral care of the parish as a whole and the community at large. 'Outreach' had become a familiar concept and the name and watchword of a valuable working group in the parish. Strong links have been forged with schools, community organisations and other churches and every attempt made to foster an atmosphere of welcoming and support among parishioners and the local community.

One important series of events needs to be chronicled here: those which led up to the decision to ordain women to the diaconate and priesthood. The Governing Body of the Church in Wales had decided in April 1975 that there was no fundamental theological objection to the ordination of women to the priesthood and in 1980 had given approval for the ordination of women to the diaconate. It was not until 1996 that the Governing Body decided to allow women deacons to proceed to the priesthood. The first ordinations took place in January 1997 when sixty-nine women from the whole province were ordained, among them the Revd. Susan Helen Jones, Anglican chaplain of the University of Wales, Swansea since 1995 and a valued member of the clergy attached to Sketty parish. She first celebrated the eucharist at St. Paul's to a packed church. All recognised this as an important event in the life of the parish.

Services at St. Paul's had been broadcast over the radio on a number of occasions but in October 1998 the church was privileged to host a diocesan live televised service at which the bishop presided. Clergy from other parishes also attended. The event marked Bishop Dewi Bridges's last act of service prior to his retirement and also coincided with the anniversary of the birthday of the diocese.

In was with great sorrow that the parish learnt in the autumn of 1999 that the vicar would shortly leave the parish. Bishop Anthony had appointed him Residentiary Canon and Director of Ministry with pastoral responsibility for Port Eynon with Rhosili, Llanddewi and Knelston. [He was appointed Archdeacon of Gower on 1st September 2000]. The parish held its official farewell and presentation to Canon Williams before choral evensong on 14th November 1999 and a special ¼ peel of bells rang out to thank him and bid him farewell.

Church Organisations

The end of an incumbency is a convenient time to review the organisations which serve the Church in its worship, which maintain its administration, promote its membership and bring parishioners and community together. It is useful to look at them at one point in time for the interest of future parishioners and local historians and provides too an opportunity to record information about them which could not have been introduced earlier without disturbing the flow of the narrative.

There have been an *organist, choir and bell-ringers* to accompany worship since the church was founded. The first organist was a Mr. Brain, a pupil of James Turle, who was organist of Westminster Abbey from 1831 to 1875. The celebrated photograph of the choir in 1877 (this is most probably the correct date, though the vestry framed copy is dated 1875 and the 1950 history has 1885) shows the organist Mr. Cryer with a choir of twenty-one members, men and boys. A former choir boy, writing in 1981, recalled that in 1923 there were seven boys on the south side and five on the north and that numbers increased when the chancel was extended in 1929 to include a full complement of men choristers, tenors on the south, baritones on the north with a number of lady choristers behind the tenors. A shortage of boy recruits was noted as early as July 1966. At the time of writing there are three boys, eleven girls, twelve women and seven men, thirty-three in all, under the direction of Dr. Ian Graham, Ph.D., FRSC, ARCO, ARCM, FTCL. He is assisted by Richard Burden, another experienced organist and church musician.

His predecessors included T.D. Jones, a well-known musician who retired at the end of 1920, J.W.V. Davies (1921-23) and Clifford H. Trotman who was appointed in 1923 and served as organist for fifty years. He was a well-known figure in the 1930s – pedalling his cycle around Sketty and Swansea, attired in breeches. He died in 1978. He was succeeded by Mr. John M. Davies, who served until 1985, and is now organist of St. Barnabas, and Mrs. Eileen Jones (formerly Evans) who preceded Dr. Graham. The last named was appointed in 1991. The original organ had been repaired, reconstructed and enlarged at various times, notably in 1923 for the now small sum of £250 and in 1963 when it was completely rebuilt by Hill, Norman and Beard for £6,000. It was eventually realised that a new organ would have to be purchased and a fund was set up for this purpose. This was augmented by a substantial legacy from Miss Marion Thomas who had died in 1993. A new Copeman Hart, three manual electronic organ was purchased in 1998 and installed in January 1999. It was dedicated on 7th February 1999 when the Bishop Elect, now Bishop Anthony, presided. The church has a vibrant musical tradition.

The *choir* sings two services each Sunday which alternate weekly between full Choral Evensong and Sung Eucharist. The church is packed for the annual Festival of Nine Lessons and Carols. The choir sings annually at Brecon Cathedral and is in demand elsewhere: during 2000 it made a much praised debut at St. David's Cathedral. For young people choir membership is seen as a valuable introduction to the concept of service in the church. Young choristers are taught not only how and when to sing but also much about the context within which they sing. Quite a few, past and present, gain qualifications – Dean's Chorister, Bishop's Chorister – awarded by the Royal School of Church Music. The choir flourishes as a recruiter of young people and has had its fair share of future clerics, these last including Andrew Knight, Sketty's present incumbent.

The *bell-ringers*, now led by Mrs. Hilary Rose as tower captain, have been in existence as a group as long as the church itself and ring out on Sundays, festivals and other special occasions of joy and sorrow in the life of the community. Nowadays they are more than a call to prayer, rather an act of witness that the Church is always there for the people. The team of twenty-two are members of the Swansea and Brecon Guild of Church Bell-ringers and have won a number of prizes over the years. At the 1999 competition the two bands entered by St. Paul's were placed first and third. They practice on Tuesday evenings and once a month with the Diocesan Guild at different towers. The *Orchestra and Singing Group* was founded in 1991 and is under the leadership of Miss Linda Chaplin, B.Ed., ALCM. Eight instrumentalists and seven singers have contributed, providing valuable support for services at St. Paul's and Holy Trinity and for church-related events outside.

The clergy are supported by ten lay *eucharistic assistants*. Eight administer the chalice at church eucharists and two lay pastoral assistants administer communion to the sick at home or in hospital. There is a flourishing *Women's Altar Flower Guild* which has thirty-three members, twenty-three of which form the weekly rota providing flowers at the altar and memorial book.

The *Parochial Church Council* is the paramount church organisation. The Revd. Lillingston formed a council in November 1906 which was described as 'a body through which the opinion of the congregation could be voiced'. It seems to have fizzled out. A surviving minute book records that the first meeting of the P.C.C. was held on 23rd January 1914. Its continuous history, however, as an institution provided for by the Constitution of the Church in Wales, dates from Disestablishment in 1920-1. The Council consists of the clergy, the churchwardens (the Vicar's Warden appointed by the vicar, the People's by the Annual Vestry meeting) and lay members over eighteen years of age also elected by the Annual Vestry. The Annual Vestry consists of those lay communicants over the age of sixteen who have been entered on the electoral roll. The function of the churchwardens, as defined by the Constitution, is to represent the laity in the parish, 'to promote peace and unity among parishioners, and by example and precept to encourage the parishioners in the practice of true religion'. The P.C.C.'s function is to meet at least four times a year and 'consult and cooperate with the incumbent in all matters of concern and importance to the parish'.

There are a number of sub-committees of the P.C.C. whose work is intimately connected with the mission of the Church. The *Caring Group Committee*, chaired by Mrs. Joyce Cole, has oversight of the needs of those who are unable, or find it difficult to attend church. It arranges house visits, shared meetings in private houses and car lifts to church when necessary. The *Renewal Committee* chaired by the vicar concerns itself with the needs of youth of the parish and how they can be better catered for. The *Training Committee* chaired by Mr. Graham Wattley takes responsibility for lay training and the development of house groups making use of the "Alpha" Course. *The World Mission and Stewardship Group*, chaired by Miss Elizabeth Rhodes, has a wider remit and deals with the mission of the church overseas and the raising of aid and relief for distressed countries such as Bosnia, Romania and Kosovo. The latter is run by Sketty Aid organised by Mr. John Steele. The work of the ecumenical movement has been mentioned earlier in this history. The main object of the *Ecumenism Committee*, chaired by Miss Joyce Phillips, is to keep the vision of Christian unity before the parish and to forge strong links with Cytun, Churches Together in Sketty. They participate in the Week of Prayer for Christian Unity, the services organised by Cytun and in the Lent House Groups. *The Fellowship Committee*, chaired by Mrs. Elaine Gale, provides opportunities for people within and outside the parish to meet informally at a programmed series of social events and also support for a number of parish functions and fund-raising activities.

The *Mothers' Union* was founded as a national society in 1876 to uphold the sanctity of marriage and develop in mothers a sense of responsibility in the training of their children. The date of the foundation of the Sketty branch cannot be pin-pointed with precision but it must have been established sometime in the latter part of the nineteenth century and has had a continuous history since. It meets regularly under the chairmanship of its branch leader Mrs. Nyra Harris.

The Churchwomen's Guild, now chaired by Mrs. Florence Thomas, has been in existence since 1947. It holds monthly meetings and slide shows, makes and repairs church kneelers, and arranges outings and Bring and Buy Sales in aid of church funds. It is complemented by *Holy Trinity Church Guild* chaired by Mrs. Audrey Milne. *Women on Wednesday*, chaired by Mrs. Carol Edwards, was started in 1988. It is a friendship society for women of all ages regardless of creed and organises talks, demonstrations and outings. With more women working at daytime jobs the crèche has become an established institution in most communities. The *Tots on Tuesdays* organised by Mrs. Vivia Jones at St. Paul's and *Holy Terrors* which meets at Holy Trinity on Thursdays and is run by Mrs. Nansi Warlow, offer something more than the secular crèche. Both aim to start proceedings with a spiritual message and to include simple Christian teaching.

The *Sunday School* is the most vital of all church institutions. It is the means by which Christian doctrine and religious knowledge is imparted to those at a period of their lives when they are most open to formative influences for good or evil and is therefore a major guarantor of the future membership of the church. Yet as an institution it has been declining in almost every church for a period of forty years. That it has survived at all is due to a succession of committed teachers. In 1963 the three Sunday Schools operating at St. Paul's, All Souls and Parklands had 120 pupils. Since then All Souls has become a separate parish and the temporary congregation at Parklands re-located at Holy Trinity Church. The Sunday School at Holy Trinity Church, which was run by Mrs. Iris Jones and had from ten to twelve pupils, was merged with that at St. Paul's about eight years ago. The present Sunday School has forty pupils on the books, of whom about twenty attend regularly. There are twelve helpers operating on a rota system. These were led by Mrs. Sue James, who has been succeeded by Mrs. Sandra Poole. Candidates for confirmation are taught separately by suitably qualified instructors. Six from the parish were confirmed in December 1999.

The 2nd Sketty (St. Paul's) *Guides* were first registered on 1st January 1920, re-registered on 9th June 1927 and has had a continuous history since. Mrs. Ann Morgan took over the unit in 1983. She had been a Brownie and Guide herself and rejoined as an Assistant Guider in 1967 when Mrs. Betty Clement was Guider. There are now fourteen guides. The *Brownies* were registered on 15th January 1921 as a GFS Brownie Unit, then re-registered on 4th March 1972. Since that date they have run continuously. Mrs. Ann Morgan joined as a leader in 1974 (when Mrs. Christine Williams was a Brownie Guider) and took over the unit in 1983. There are now twenty-seven Brownies. The *Rainbows* (Baby Brownies) were registered on 15th November 1991 and have been run by Mrs. Wendy Phelan as Guider since their inception. They number from eighteen to twenty.

The 44th Swansea (St. Paul's) *Scout Group* was registered in 1942 and at first had *Cubs* only. The two packs of Cubs numbering fifty-two are now run by Mrs. Vivienne Lewis with three warranted helpers. She took over from Mrs. Sylvia Walker in 1969. The *Scouts* were started in 1956 and are now run by Mr. Alan Mone who took over from Mr. Mike Phippen two years ago. There are eighteen of them. In May 1999 they were awarded £134,716 by the National Lottery Charities Board towards the cost of re-building their dilapidated Gower Road headquarters.

Church-sponsored *youth clubs* have had a checkered history, partly because the parish is within the catchment areas of two high-achieving schools which themselves provide a variety of recreational activities in the evenings. However, a church youth club was re-formed in September 1997 by Revd. Susan Jones, the Anglican University chaplain, with numbers fluctuating between four and twelve. As an 18+ group it was run by the Revd. Martin Batchelor following the departure of Revd. Susan Jones in September 1998 to take up the appointment of Director of Pastoral Studies at St. Michael's College, Llandaff. As 'New Sketty' it is now organised by Revd. Jenny Wigley. Numbers fluctuate between four and fifteen. The group meets twice a month on Sunday evenings for discussions, prayer sessions and social events.

Curates from St. Mary's had ministered on the university campus in the late 1950s and early 1960s but the *Anglican chaplaincy* was not really established until the appointment of the Revd. Graham Chadwick in 1963. The chaplaincy has only been officially attached to Sketty parish since 1995. Since student numbers have now topped the 10,000 mark, the link with what must be the highest concentration of young men and women in the city is an important one.

Among the oldest of the church clubs with a continuous history is the *Sketty Church Cricket Club*. Founded in 1890, it owed much of its early success to the leadership of an enthusiastic curate of St. Paul's, Revd. Norman Parcell (1909-24). In 1990 the club published *Sketty Church Cricket Club: 100 not out: Centenary Year 1890-1990*, an evocative collection of reminiscences and photographs. It played its first game on its new ground at Upper Killay in 1992.

Sharing honours for longevity with the Mothers' Union and the Sketty Church Cricket Club, special mention needs to be made of the parish magazine, *The Beacon*. The purpose of a parish magazine was aptly defined by a former Archdeacon of Gower, Harold Stepney Williams, when he started his own magazine at Oystermouth in 1899: 'to chronicle local events, and to be a means of communication between clergy and people. By means of this publication we shall be able to make known what has been done, what is being done, and what is intended to be done'. St. Paul's, Sketty had a joint publication with Cocket starting at an unknown date until 1905. In that year the Revd. G.C. Lillingston started a separate publication. It changed its appearance and format over the years but was continuously printed commercially by Crown Printers, Morriston, except for periods during World War II. In January 1977 it merged with a publication produced by Holy Trinity Youth Club and became *The Beacon*. Thereafter it was produced by duplicate typing and more recently by more modern computer methods. The magazine had originally been edited by the vicar but *The Beacon* was first edited by Mr. Walter Hume and Mrs. Julia Mitchell, then by Mr. Walter Hunt followed by Mr. A.K. Cole who sadly died in 1997. His successor as editor, Stuart Ball, also died suddenly and the magazine was edited on a temporary basis by the Revd. Martin Batchelor with the help of David Heap. It is now edited by Rachel and David Bould, with Kathryn and Trevor Sperring. The magazine is something more than a means of communication. It is an invaluable record of parish life for the future historian and needs to be bound and treasured. It was a great blow to the writer of the present history, and doubtless to many parishioners, to learn that the file of the magazine before 1959 had been irretrievably lost.

Most church organisations have interrupted histories. Some become defunct; some experience difficulty in recruiting suitable leaders and organisers, others yet again change their form or title. The *Church Lads Brigade* began as a cadet organisation attached to the Kings Royal Rifles and had a flourishing group at St. Paul's early in the twentieth century started by Vicar Akrill-Jones (1909-15). A number of its members served in World War I but it now seems part of our imperial past and will certainly remain defunct. Among those in abeyance or absorbed into other organisations are the *Church of England Men's Society*, the *Girls Friendly Society* (both founded by Vicar Akrill-Jones) and more recently *Cymry'r Groes* and *Servants of the Sanctuary*.

St. Paul's has been extremely fortunate in having a fund of dedicated and talented parishioners who have been able to maintain a rich social life in the parish. The Revd. Garfield James wrote plaintively in the parish magazine in 1964 that 'he could not recall a time when the parochial organisations were more active . . . though their strength was by no means adequately reflected in attendance at church'. It is a perennial complaint of the clergy. Yet in an age of falling church attendances every link with the wider community, however tenuous, should be valued and cultivated.

CHAPTER 4

Church Extension

St. Martin's, Dunvant and St. Hilary's, Killay

The term 'church extension' was coined by the Victorians to describe a movement not only for enlarging the physical structure of existing churches but for providing additional church accommodation in the form of mission halls and daughter churches to cater for the needs of a rapidly increasing population. It was a movement closely linked with the provision of additional pastoral superintendence through the appointment of assistant curates. The parish of St. Paul's Sketty, as we have seen, was carved out of the parish of St. Mary's, Swansea. It was not an urgently needed act of church extension because Sketty at this time was no more than a small village at a cross-roads. But by the 1860s a more concentrated settlement of working class housing began to grow along the western and north western edge of the parish at Killay and Dunvant. Collieries had been operating on this western edge of the Glamorgan coalfield since medieval times but industrialists were now expecting more substantial returns and deeper seams were being explored and exploited and the coal carried out on a branch tramway line of the Mumbles Railway. In the early 1860s a more extensive railway link was being forged with Swansea. Railway navvies were excavating the route and laying the track of a railway extension across the neck of the Gower peninsula from Pontardulais down the Clyne Valley to Blackpill and thence eastward along the sea front ending in what became Victoria Station, Swansea. This railway gave Swansea a direct link with central Wales and the north of England and, with stations at Killay and Dunvant, reinforced this industrial part of Sketty parish.

The Revd. E.G. Williams declared in his pamphlet *Move on!* that Montague Earle Welby, St. Paul's second incumbent, 'was most active and industrious, building a church room at Killay for the purpose of lectures and a Sunday School'. The school became the special concern of the Dillwyns of Hendrefoilan House. In 1857 Welby married Mary Dillwyn, a daughter of Lewis Weston Dillwyn. Her niece, Elizabeth Amy Dillwyn, then in her late teens, took on the task of teaching the forty odd children there. Amy recorded in her diary that they spat on their slates to clean

St. Hilary's Church
(J. Beynon)

them, used their pinafores to blow their noses and that their dirty clothes smelt to high heaven in hot weather. 'Oh dear', she wrote, 'I think trying to civilize Killay is very hard work, and perhaps . . . all work to no purpose especially when people begin to talk of having a policeman at Killay because of its being so uproarious'. The *Commercial Inn* first opened its doors in October 1849 and it was near here that the 1866 cholera epidemic first struck in Killay. Amy Dillwyn courageously risked her own health in visiting and tending the sick during the epidemic. By this time Revd. E.W. Bolney had succeeded Welby at St. Paul's. Any cooperative venture with Bolney must have been difficult for Amy for she did not like him. He read the services too slowly, she complained, and pestered her with proposals of marriage. He claimed eventually that he would remain single as long as she did and kept his word. Both died unmarried.

In 1886 the first services were held in the tiny three-roomed church school in Killay, where Amy had taught, and were taken by two laymen F.S. Bishop and R.G. Cawker (who was a churchwarden of St. James in 1884) on alternate Sundays. In 1897 a small, corrugated iron mission church was built near the junction of Goetre Fawr and Dunvant Roads on a site long since covered by housing. It cost £500 to build. Bishop John Owen came down to dedicate and consecrate the church to St. Martin of Tours on the saint's feast day, 11th November 1897. From 1897 the church was served by a succession of curates: D. Price (1897-1901), Lewis Davies (1901-8), Gwilym Smith (1908-10), Ll. P. Rees (1910-14), D.D. Jones (1914-19) and D. Eustace Jones (1918-21). These were almost certainly the earliest assistant clergy appointed to Sketty, with financial help from the Additional Curates Society. By this time the congregation was dwindling and the temporary church really needed replacing with a more durable structure. When the Sketty curate the Revd. D. Lynne Davies was put in charge in 1921 he preached to a congregation of twelve and this included three small boys who made up the choir. The corrugated roof leaked – the sky was visible through it – and there was no heating system.

The vicar of St. Paul's, the Revd. H.J. Stewart and his curate, had now to plan for a new church. D. Lynne Davies, on the advice of his churchwardens at St. Martin's, acquired the cooperation of Mr. Bound, Station Master of Dunvant, to help drum up support for the church. The first church fête held in 1921 brought in £210 towards the New Church Building Fund. In 1922 the churchyard was purchased and consecrated by Bishop Owen on his last visit as diocesan to Swansea. The church school in Gower Road where Amy Dillwyn had taught, vandalised and long disused, was now repaired and used for Sunday School and evensong and local Sketty ordinands, among them Leslie Norman, Ieuan Davies and Bill Bromham, helped with the services. In 1924 the old parish hall was renovated but the main object still remained – the building of a new church. Some £5000 had already been raised when the foundation stone of St. Hilary's was laid in 1925. In October of the same year the independent parish of Killay came into existence, with Revd. Lynne Davies as its first vicar and Mr. W.J. Bound and Mr. W. Diment as the first churchwardens. The church was dedicated to St. Hilary (*c.*315-*c.*368), teacher and mentor of St. Martin of Tours. Mr. Bound, on promotion, moved and resigned as vicar's warden, to be replaced by another railwayman, Mr. John Powell. As the compilers of the Jubilee brochure remark, St. Hilary's connection with the railway was important, 'stationmaster, signalman, superintendent of the line: all participated equally in the early history of the parish of Killay'. With the creation of the new parish, St. Paul's, Sketty ceased to have responsibility for Killay and Dunvant. The new church designed by Glendinning Moxham, was consecrated by Bishop Edward L. Bevan, first bishop of Swansea and Brecon diocese, on 10th August 1926.

All Souls, Carnglas

The population of Sketty trebled in the first half of this century, growing from 2,700 in 1901 to 8,721 in 1951. Even before the beginning of the century the town of Swansea in its expansion westward had been reaching out with ribbon development through Walter Rd., with St. Mary's new chapel of ease at St. James (1867), to the village and church of Sketty. The electric tram service from Swansea had reached Sketty in 1910. But it was in the inter war years that Sketty received its greatest accretion of population, with the old farmlands being sold off for housing development and a concentrated pattern of roads and streets appearing to the north and north-west of the church and almost a new suburb emerging at Tycoch and Carnglas. In 1932 a notice board was erected on what is now Tycoch Square, bearing the words 'Site for new daughter church for Sketty'. These were the years of depression and unemployment followed by the outbreak of the war in 1939. The departure of the vicar, Chancellor Stewart, in 1941 meant that plans for the new church had to be shelved. His successor, Canon J. Gwyn Davies, however, revived the project and began raising funds. The old site had long since been sold off and on 5th August 1944 a new site was purchased from the Morris estate for £200. It lay on the south side of Hendrefoilan Road. By 1946 when

Interior of All Souls, Carnglas
(P. J. Gwynn)

Canon Davies left to become Dean of Monmouth, the sum of £3,000 had already been raised. It had been his ambition to see the church built and dedicated to All Souls. It would, he declared in his farewell letter, 'meet the spiritual needs of those who literally cannot come to the parish church, but also commemorate the greatest crisis in our history and those who gave their lives that we might live'.

The difficulties of Revd. J. Hill's vicariate (1946-50) delayed progress but the new vicar, the Revd. Harry Williams, nudged by his archdeacon, Harold Stepney Williams, (who had a proven record of church extension in his old parish of Oystermouth), took up the work again. He realised that much money would have to be raised but that, more importantly, he would have to lay the necessary spiritual foundations. That would mean starting and building a Sunday School. Intensive visiting in the Carnglas area revealed that a number of children were attending the local Baptist Sunday School even though they had been baptised in St. Paul's – the church and the Stewart Hall were too far away. A room was rented in the Sketty Junior School on Tycoch Square and two of St. Paul's most experienced teachers, Jack and Dorothy Hunter, volunteered to take charge of the venture. When the school was opened at 2.30 p.m. on Sunday 19th April 1953 only five children turned up. Numbers grew, week by week, and on Mothering Sunday 28th March 1954, the school hall was full of parents and children assembled for a special service. The school was now thriving with five Sunday School teachers. Meanwhile thanks to Cyril A. Hughes, architect (a member of St. Paul's P.C.C. who was to become vicar's warden in 1955) a new and better site was found for the church on a vacant plot between Harlech Crescent and Hendrefoilan Road. After negotiations with the Spragg Estate and the Swansea Corporation, the ground was leased in October 1954 to the Representative Body of the Church in Wales at an annual rent of £1 with permission to build a church and vicarage on it. Both Cyril Hughes and Basil Ellis, a chartered quantity surveyor, who was secretary to the P.C.C., gave their services free of charge in drawing up the working drawings and plans. The tender of Griffith Davies & Co. Ltd. was accepted in February 1956 to build the church for £18,292. On 9th May 400 people gathered to witness the Ven. J.J.A. Thomas, archdeacon of Gower, plant a cross on the spot where the altar was to stand. He declared that while steps were being taken to demolish the remains of the blitzed church of Holy Trinity, Swansea, the new church of All Souls would arise at Carnglas. The vicar now launched an appeal for £10,000 to build the church. On 27th June 350 people processed from Sketty School, Tycoch Square with Bishop Glyn Simon to see him lay the foundation stone and take part in a service on site. In the winter of 1956-57 Sketty members of the Church of England Men's Society visited each house in the Carnglas area with a letter from the vicar giving information on the new church which was now rapidly nearing completion. Built of pale brown brick and roofed with dark pantiles, it embodies, to use the words of the late Professor Roy Knight, the church's historian, 'the qualities the architect sought to achieve – dignity, proportion, simplicity'. A lofty building combining nave and chancel in the modern manner, it has an open bell-tower on the south side containing a tenor bell, a replica of one at St. Paul's. A stone statue of St. Michael weighing souls on the day of judgement, bearing in his hand the flaming sword of justice surmounts the entrance porch. It was not carved out of the solid but a wooden mould was carved to the architect's specification and a cast made *in situ*. The long vertical windows of clear glass give a strong feeling of light, space and repose. There is no east window but an embroidered hanging of Christ in glory over the altar. The ceiling is of pale blue coffering, bordered with gold and red and framed in deeper blue. There are no side chapels and no carved wood except for the pulpit crucifix. The altar is of silver grey Scotch marble and was unfortunately put in position before the liturgical innovations of the 1960s when the free standing altar with the priest facing the congregation became more acceptable. The church building had cost £19,363, the furnishings £1,063, and the organ £1,587. Towards the total of £22,013 Sketty Parish Building Fund had contributed £11,998 and the Church in Wales £3,000. The Church was dedicated by Bishop Glyn Simon on 12th September 1957 and the first regular service held on 15th September. As a daughter church, it continued to be served by the vicar of St. Paul's (from 1958 Revd. Garfield H. James) and his assistant curates, successively Ronald H. Lloyd, Samuel Rhys Griffith, Dudley W. White, and John A.M. Jenkins. They virtually became priests-in-charge. From the beginning a sung parish eucharist was the sole Sunday morning service. 'All Souls,' wrote Professor Roy Knight, 'had been born at the right time to be influenced by the renewed emphasis in the Church on the Holy Eucharist and from the beginning a sung parish eucharist has been the sole Sunday morning service, uniting virtually the whole parish every week in one corporate act of worship – to the exclusion of matins, and also, it must be said, to the great detriment of evensong, which has never held with us the place it once held at Sketty.' More surprisingly, liturgical vestments were adopted at All Souls, while at St. Paul's the vicar still celebrated in surplice. The seeds for this innovation were probably sown when the All Souls Women's Club visited Margam Abbey. The vicar of Margam, the Revd. E.A. Munro Cape, took a particular delight in displaying the vestments to visitors, especially those presented to the church by Father Arthur Stanton, the Anglo-Catholic curate of St. Alban's, Holborn and the *bête noire* of Bishop Ollivant of Llandaff. Stanton had been forbidden to celebrate or preach in his diocese. In the parish congregational meeting of 1965 the Revd. Garfield James remarked with a smile that All Souls had gone in for 'warmth and colour' because overhead heating as well as liturgical vestments had been introduced. The first set of eucharistic vestments was presented to the church by the Women's Club. All Souls shed its dependent status and became a separate parish in 1972 and the Revd. D.E. Paul Wilkinson was instituted and inducted as the first incumbent on 24th November.

Holy Trinity, Sketty Park

The population of Sketty, rather surprisingly, remained static throughout the greater part of the 1950s. In the late 1950s, however, part of the old Sketty Park estate was purchased by the Corporation from Armine Morris. The southern part was designated for private building and the northern for council ownership with a provision of houses for renting. When the estate was laid out a place for a church centre was reserved. It was to be a dual-purpose building designed to serve as a place of worship and as a meeting place for social events and, it was estimated, would cost at least £17,000 to build. An appeal for money towards the building of the new church was launched by Bishop J.J.A. Thomas on 30th January 1966. Cyril Hughes, parishioner and professional architect, again volunteered to give his services, which would otherwise have cost the parish over £1,000, free of charge. On 12th September 1967 Bishop Glyn Simon planted a Cross on the spot where the altar of the new church was to stand and on 18th March 1968 on a cold rough evening the same bishop laid the church's foundation stone which had been quarried in the Forest of Dean. Building now began in earnest. The usual strategy had been adopted to lay the spiritual foundations of the church. A room in Parklands School had been hired, at first for a Sunday School under the leadership of Mrs. Nellie Francis and Mr. Peter Willcocks, and later for a monthly celebration of the eucharist as well. The new church and furnishings ultimately cost £22,000. On 2nd June 1969 the bishop processed with a large contingent of clergy, choir and parishioners in driving rain from Parklands School to the new church and dedicated it to the Holy Trinity. On 8th June the bishop celebrated the first Sunday eucharist there. Unlike St. Hilary's, Killay and All Souls, Carnglas, Holy Trinity has remained a daughter church dependent on St. Paul's and served by its clergy.

CHAPTER 5

Church Fabric and Furnishings

The church which Bishop Thirlwall dedicated in 1850 has been described in the first chapter. In the succeeding one hundred and fifty years, it has been enlarged, altered and enriched in response to practical needs, changing fashions and generous benefactors. Thanks to the lucid plans drawn up by the late Cyril Hughes, the surviving faculties (the ecclesiastical equivalents of planning permission) and other records, it is possible to chronicle the major changes in some detail.

Additions During the Vicariate of E.W. Bolney

The first major ornamental addition to the church was made in 1878 when a reredos of the Last Supper with figures and furniture in relief was erected behind the high altar. It was the gift of Sarah Vivian, widow of John Henry Vivian. In the correspondence attached to the faculty granting permission for its erection, it was noted that the Chancellor had objected to the word 'altar' in the petition, an indication of how sensitive members of the ecclesiastical establishment were at this time towards anything that smacked of popery or ritualism. About the same time Mrs. Averil Vivian had presented the fine brass lectern to the church in memory of her father who had died in 1870 and her brother who had died in 1877.

In August 1889 a fine clock weighing 15 cwt. was affixed to the north side of the church tower. It was the gift of Aubrey Vivian (1854-98), the second and, despite their differing religious opinions, favourite son of Henry Hussey Vivian.

In the same year the Revd. E.G. Williams in a pamphlet on church progress in Swansea (*Move on!*) noted that Mr. Bolney had 'recently built an additional wing to the church'. It was something more than a wing. Cyril Hughes' second plan of the church shows that the old vestry and organ loft adjoining the sanctuary to the south was taken down and a new, enlarged, one-story vestry rebuilt to replace it. The 'wing' referred to by E.G. Williams was built as a new organ loft north of, and with access to, the choir stalls in the chancel. Why were these alterations deemed necessary? The answer seems to lie in the need for a robing area when surplices were introduced in place of the Eton jackets and waistcoats regularly supplied by Mrs. Sarah Vivian until her death in 1886. When they wore the livery designed by Mrs. Vivian they came to church already dressed for choir and there was no need for a robing room. With the introduction of the surplice extra space was needed for storage and for robing, hence the new extensions. The new 1889 extension was not designed to provide extra accommodation for the ordinary non-choir members of the congregation.

Between 1899-1900 a major transformation of the sanctuary area took place when a fine set of mosaics were placed on either side of the reredos. They are described in detail in the next chapter.

The Building of the North Aisle, 1908

In 1907 Revd. Lillingston called in the local architect Glendinning Moxham to draw up preliminary plans for the building of a north aisle. He also applied to the Incorporated Church Building Society for grant aid. In his application form Lillingston noted that the 1901 population of Sketty was 2,700 and had by 1907 risen to an estimated 4,000. Three quarters of this number, he noted, were of the poorer classes whose menfolk were engaged either in the manufacturing industries or as shop assistants. The Dunvant iron church with 200 free seats catered for only 500 of this population and was two miles from St. Paul's. This left an estimated 3,500 people in Sketty proper for which St. Paul's could provide 284 seats (exclusive of seating in the chancel), of which only about 90 were free. If a north aisle was added at an estimated cost of £1,500 it would provide an additional 152 free seats. Lillingston had already raised £100 but if the fees of an architect and the salary of a clerk of the works were added to the estimated cost there would still be a deficit of £1,530. A correspondence now began with the consulting architects of the I.C.B.S. who picked holes in Moxham's plans and suggested improvements. Eventually after a good deal of give and take the plans were conditionally approved by the I.C.B.S. architects on 21st November 1907. On 17th December 1907, however, Lillingston wrote to the I.C.B.S. that 'a generous friend has promised to defray the cost of enlarging the church, so that we shall not now require the aid of the Church Building Society . . .' The generous friend was Richard Glynn Vivian (1836-1910), younger brother of Henry Hussey. He was the black sheep of the family, now blind 'by reason of his sins some said'. He contributed £1,200 and the remaining £600 of the eventual cost was collected by the villagers of Sketty.

The completed aisle was dedicated on 13th September 1908 and the brass plate attached to the wall to commemorate the gift bears an appropriate inscription from Isaiah XXXV, 5: 'the eyes of the blind shall be opened and the ears of the deaf unstopped'.

The New Vicarage, The World War I Memorial and New Lighting, 1920

In 1920 the Revd. H.J. Stewart sold the old vicarage and built the present vicarage conveniently near the church. At this time too the memorial to the seventy-four men from Sketty who gave their lives in World War I was affixed to the wall of the north aisle. It was designed by Glendinning Moxham, sculpted by W.E. Brown, Gower St., Swansea, and unveiled at an armistice service on 11th November 1920. Electric light appears to have been introduced into the church and church hall between 1922 and 1924 when payments for electricity instead of gas appear in the churchwardens' accounts.

The Chancel Extended and the Chancel Arch Widened, 1928-29

Stewart now proposed to extend the chancel and vestries and widen the chancel arch and asked the architect Glendinning Moxham to submit preliminary plans. He also invited Sir Charles Nicholson to come down to Sketty and give his views on what was proposed. Sir Charles Nicholson (1867-1949) was a former pupil of the architect J.D. Sedding and during a distinguished career had been appointed consulting architect to seven cathedrals including Llandaff. His report has survived in the archives of the Incorporated Church Building Society now at Lambeth Palace Library. In it Sir Charles first paid tribute to the excellence of the work of the original architect of the church 'which appears to me to be one of the best works of its period'. He did not know the name of the architect was Woodyer but observed that 'his work was obviously done under the influence of Pugin and the Ecclesiological Society and reproduced the feeling of an old village church with considerable success'. He adduced three reasons why the chancel should be lengthened. The existing chancel was inconveniently small for practical purposes; it required enlarging to restore the original relative proportions of the church since it had been enlarged by the building of the north aisle. Thirdly, Sir Charles had little doubt that the original architect would have built a longer chancel 'if the conditions of 1850 had allowed him to do so'. The plan to extend the

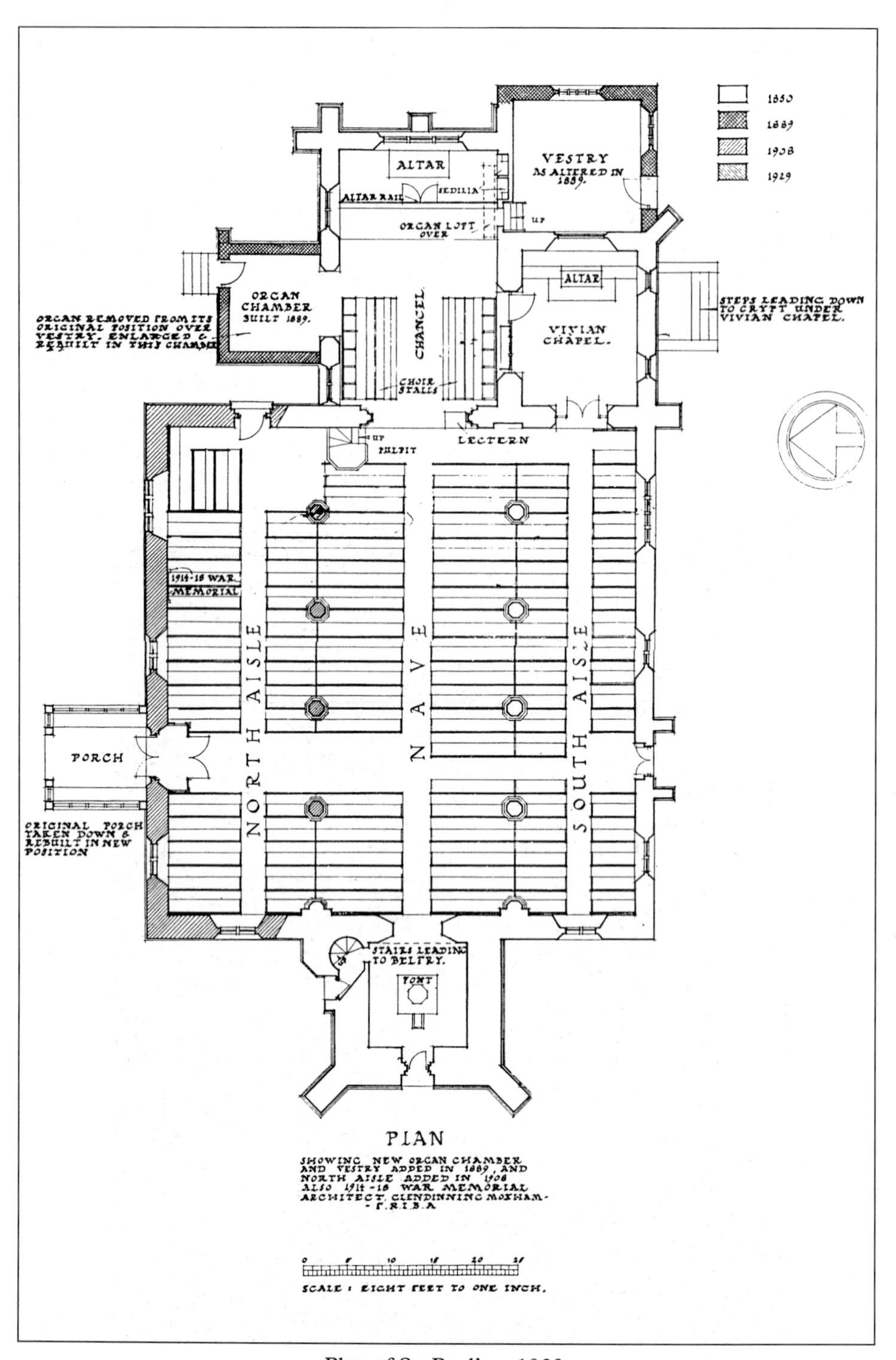

Plan of St. Paul's, *c.*1929

(St. Paul's Church Archives/West Glamorgan Record Office)

north aisle eastwards and to place the organ on a loft was a sound one, acoustically and visually. The floor levels in the chancel should not be raised more than can be helped because the chancel wall was already low. 'It would be an advantage', he added, 'to raise the back row of seats in the chancel on a platform keeping the boys' seats on the floor'. The widening and raising of the chancel arch would be a great advantage 'from a practical point of view, and will, I think, be an artistic improvement'. He was pleased that they proposed using stone for the chancel floor and that the altar was to be lengthened slightly. 'From our conversation', he concluded, 'I gather we are in complete agreement as to the desirability of obtaining as much light as possible in the sanctuary and that you have an open mind as to retaining the little stone gallery over the present sedilia'.

John Newman in his account of St. Paul's in *Buildings of Wales: Glamorgan*, p.618, mentions that the chancel is 'dominated by the extraordinary

St. Paul's Chancel
(J. Beynon)

stone canopy over the sedilia'. It is not in fact a canopy but the elaborately carved gallery which once fronted the organ loft adjoining the chancel. The organ loft was sealed off and a new one placed in a north wing added to the chancel by Bolney in 1889. The ornamental front of the gallery was retained in its position over the sedilia even when the chancel was extended in 1929.

Mrs. John Glasbrook had already undertaken to pay for the enlargement of the chancel and vestries and the provision of a new east window at a cost of nearly £4,000. It was to be a memorial to her husband who had been vicar's warden for many years. To extend the north aisle and take down the organ chamber, Stewart needed an extra £1,800. He now applied to the Incorporated Church Building Society for assistance and pointed out that the population of Sketty was now about 5,500, about one half of which were poor and nearly all the others suffering through the depression in trade. 'It is the very worst time I remember', wrote Stewart, 'in my experience of Swansea during the past thirty years. We are also face to face with considerable expenditure on our day schools.' The church was given the small grant of £60 by the I.C.B.S. but by this time local subscribers had also rallied to help the building fund and the outstanding deficit was cleared before the new east window was dedicated on 1st March 1929. The whole extension and widening of the chancel arch had been completed before the vestry meeting of 9th April 1929. The years of depression and the outbreak of war in 1939 put a stop to any major work on the fabric but money was found for one small undertaking. The Children's Corner was a fashionable addition to churches at this time and on 6th June 1940 the vicar and churchwardens obtained a faculty to install a children's chapel with altar and altar rails and other facilities for a children's corner at the east end of the north aisle. The work was inspired largely by Mrs. Stewart, the vicar's wife and was completed to plans and designs prepared by Messrs. Mercer and Vaughan, Architects, Wind St., Swansea. It was consecrated on 9th September 1940. The moving of the furniture from the corner to the back of the church to enable the Revd. J.C. Hill to celebrate an early Sunday eucharist there was to be the occasion of one of the early skirmishes between that incumbent and a number of his parishioners.

World War II Memorial, 1952

The uncertainties and austerities of the wartime and post-war period and the need to put money aside for the projected new church at Carnglas put a further curb on improvements to the fabric of St. Paul's. On 1st

April 1952, however, a faculty was obtained to erect an oak panel on the east wall of the Children's or Lady Chapel and inscribe on it the names of Sketty men and women who had been killed in the second world war. This was really a preliminary tribute, for the future All Souls church was to be the monument to the ultimate sacrifice they had made. The faculty also gave permission for an oak screen to be erected between the Children's or Lady Chapel and the nave, and another between the chapel and the chancel. The new work was dedicated by Bishop Williamson on 4th November 1952 and commemorated the names of the 101 Sketty men and women who had been killed in the war.

The New High Altar, 1955

The fine stone high altar with a *mensa* of white travertine marble bearing the five consecration crosses and a three panel frontal of blue marble, was designed and erected by Cyril Hughes as a memorial to his wife, Edna Laura, who died on 26th November 1954, and it was dedicated on 19th May (Ascension Day) 1955. The central panel bears the sacred monogram IHS: Iesus Hominum Salvator: Jesus Saviour of Mankind. The brass cross and candlesticks which adorned the earlier altar are still used on this altar. They were given in memory of Charles H. Eden as 'a thanksgiving for countless blessings'.

Additions to the Baptistry and Canopies for the Clergy Stalls, 1958-59

The baptistry was refurbished in 1958. The design was undertaken by Cyril A. Hughes and Sons whose services, as hitherto, were given free of charge. The work entailed the erection of decorated panels on the interior base of the tower to accommodate on the south side the names of churchwardens of the parish and on the north side the names of the incumbents. To these years belongs too the fitting of the canopies over the clergy stalls; the one in commemoration of Elizabeth Jane Crouch, Pasadena, Sketty 16th June 1955, the other for a remembrance of William Henry Crouch, Pasadena, 18th May 1959.

Reroofing the Church, 1983-87

In a report to the P.C.C. in 1975 Cyril Hughes, the honorary church architect, had drawn attention to the serious defects which had developed in the roofing of the church, by then a hundred and twenty-six years old. The roof battens were rotting, the nails securing these to the roof beams were in a perished condition and the complete absence of any underfelting produced the frequent draughts felt by the congregation. A further report in 1977 pointed out the unusual nature of the roofing material. Tiles were used on the outer slopes and a combination of tiles and slates on the inner slopes. The Bridgewater tiles used were of soft clay and most of them were found to be scaling as a result of years of frosts and heavy rains. The inner slopes were the most affected. Nothing was done in the closing years of Garfield James's vicariate but his successor, the Revd. Luther Thomas, realised that the work could no longer be postponed. In 1982 Mr. J. Alan Hughes, who had succeeded his father as honorary church architect, prepared a detailed specification for the reroofing work for submission to five firms of local contractors. By November 1982 it was realised that the work would cost at least £40,000. The church was now embarking on, to use the vicar's words, 'the most demanding financial project that the parish has ever had to face'. Meanwhile the memory of Cyril Hughes was honoured when the bishop came down to dedicate two churchwardens chairs presented by Mr. and Mrs. Alan Hughes and Mr. and Mrs. Bryan Roberts and their families. A Reroofing Appeals Committee was set up under the chairmanship of Mr. Edwin Clement and by April 1983 appeal letters were being delivered by the Scouts and Cubs to every house in the parish. By August work had started on the south side of the chancel roof. The entire work took four years to complete at a cost of £78,334, far more than was estimated before work started. Many parishioners worked extremely hard in raising money and a number of schemes were devised, among them the novel one of selling the old copper nails from the roof produced at the Hafod works. These were inscribed with the original Vivian mark, V. & S. Parishioners and non-church people contributed generously to the appeals fund. A special tribute needs to be paid to the vicar. He was tireless in tracking down sources of grant for the work and was particularly successful in obtaining a very substantial grant from the Welsh Office (this was before the setting up of CADW), the first time such a grant had been made in Wales for the restoration of a Victorian church. A special thanksgiving choral eucharist for the successful completion of the church reroofing and restoration was celebrated by Bishop Benjamin Vaughan on 24th May 1987 which was attended by the Mayor and Mayoress and other notabilities.

Late in the same year the church received a fine moveable altar for the sanctuary, the gift of the Altar Flower Guild, and was accompanied by matching candlesticks given by Mrs. Phyl. Evans in memory of her husband Denzil. New liturgical practice required the celebrant to face the congregation during the eucharist; the new altar was therefore used at the

11 a.m. Sunday eucharist, reserving the immovable stone high altar for the 8 a.m. Sunday eucharist and high occasions.

The Spire

The spire of St. Paul's has always been regarded as a beautiful landscape feature. Its height, however – 120 feet above ground level – makes it particularly vulnerable to the effects of wind, rain and lightning and hardly an incumbency passes without some repair work needing to be done to it. In 1923 during H.J. Stewart's incumbency the original shingle on the spire was removed and replaced with slate at a cost of £600. The next major work occurred in 1974 during Garfield James's incumbency, when, during a heavy storm, the lightning conductor sprang loose and the slating suffered heavy damage. The appeal for money to pay for the repair brought a generous response from non-church people as well as from parishioners. In 1995 the weathercock was taken down, cleaned and regilded. A rolling programme of maintenance and repair organised by the vicar and church officers continues. This programme has also provided an opportunity to improve access for the disabled by raising the level of the path leading to the south aisle entrance.

Sale of the Stewart Hall Complex, 1989 and Opening of the New Parish Centre, 1992

Archdeacon Ilar Roy Luther Thomas towards the end of his vicariate at St. Paul's was often teased that he would be remembered not for the work of reroofing the church but for selling off the Stewart Hall complex. The front part of this complex was Woodyer's Gothic style church school built for the Vivians in 1853. It consisted of two classrooms and a headmaster's residence and continued to be used as a school until 1930 when the Parochial Church Council decided it had become too costly to repair and maintain as a school if it was to meet the standards required by the education authorities. It became instead the Church Institute and was used by church organisations for their meetings and events. The P.C.C. had toyed with the idea of selling the school and its site in the 1930s. Had they done so it would have become the site of the Maxime Cinema (opened November 1938) and later the Odeon Bingo Hall, now opposite. When in 1937 the P.C.C. decided to make a presentation to Canon H.J. Stewart to mark his twenty-one years of service in the parish, he generously gave the sum collected towards the building of a new church hall –

St. Paul's from south-east
(J. Beynon)

the old one, built in 1906 on Gower Road above Sketty Cross, is now occupied by the Seventh Day Adventists. The new hall was built at the rear of the school/church institute and opened in 1938 as the Stewart Hall. In subsequent years it served the parish well as a meeting place for its organisations and as a source of income from rentals.

In the 1970s and 1980s, however, the benefits of the facility were becoming less clear. The building of the Sketty Park estate brought a marked increase in traffic which made traipsing across the road from church to hall a hazard. This hazard was increased when the road through Sketty became for many the most convenient way to reach the newly-built M4. Equally worrying were the quibbles with outside organisations over the level of rentals and the escalating costs of maintenance and repair. In 1984 Dr. Graham Humphrys, Chairman of the Financial Committee, declared that 'to put matters right and make the complex as it should be would cost £100,000!' The same committee later estimated that the future annual deficit on the complex would be £5,000 which would have to come from reserves. In 1988 the vicar and the P.C.C. made the realistic but, for some, unpopular decision to close the complex and put it up for auction. For the time being more use was to be made of the church vestry, the back of the church and Holy Trinity Hall for meetings. When the Stewart Hall complex was disposed of, 'a permanent replacement was to be considered, less costly to run and more suited to present and future needs'. The site and buildings were sold at auction on 22nd August 1989 for £180,000. The net proceeds of the sale were placed on deposit at high interest rates to provide £220,000 towards the cost of a new hall. This new parish centre was built within the church grounds early in the vicariate of Revd. Stephen Brooks at a cost of £240,000. It was opened by Bishop Dewi Bridges on Easter Day, 19th April 1992 at 6.30 p.m. in the presence of the former Bishop, Benjamin Vaughan and his wife, the Lord Mayor and Lady Mayoress of the City and 300 parishioners.

The Vivian Chapel and Family Vault

The Vivian chapel has been reserved for separate treatment for its memorials belong to several periods. The chapel formed part of Woodyer's original design. It was sealed off from the chancel by a wooden screen (with door) which spanned the space below a chamfered arch, enriched with ball flower decoration. It was sealed off, too, from the south aisle by a wooden screen with a central double-doored entrance. The east end is fitted with two stone gabled canopies, richly decorated in Decorated style with crockets and cusped undersides. The canopies rest on pillars and form two recesses over imitation tomb chests which are capped with variegated black, white and red marble slabs. The fronts of these tomb chests have panels decorated with heraldic devices and shields of the Vivian family, the left one in colour, the right one plain but designed to be coloured. The whole dates from 1854, is Woodyer's work and was erected for John Henry Vivian.

On the wall of the left hand recess are affixed brass memorial plates with inscriptions copied from monuments in Truro parish church which commemorate John Henry Vivian's parents and brothers who were interred in the family vault there: John Vivian, d. 7th Dec. 1826; Betsy, his wife, d. 7th Mar. 1816; Lt. General Richard Hussey, Baron Vivian of Glynn and Truro, d. 1842 and Thomas Vivian, d. 13th Sept. 1821.

Below this is a tablet in memory of Violet Averil Margaret, eldest daughter of 1st Baron Swansea, wife of Brig. General Douglas Campbell Douglas, d. 30th March 1943.

On the wall of the right hand recess are similar brass tablets commemorating John Henry Vivian, d. 10th Feb. 1855, Sarah, his wife, d. 8th Sept. 1886, their son Henry Hussey Vivian, d. 28th Nov. 1894, and the latter's

Pietro Tenerani Monument to Jessie Dalrymple Vivian
(Crown Copyright: Royal Commission on Ancient and Historical Monuments in Wales)

third wife, Averil, d. 14th Jan. 1934. A number of the tablets contain detailed biographical details not noted here.

On the south wall of the chapel, to the right of the first window are two separate brass tablets commemorating Henry Hussey Vivian, son of the 1st Baron Swansea and Averil, his third wife, d. 11th Dec. 1898 and Richard Glynn Vivian of Sketty Hall, 4th son of J.H. Vivian, d. 7th June 1910.

Between these tablets is the large, white marble figure of a winged angel with a child playing at its feet, sculpted by Pietro Tenerani, to commemorate Jessie Dalrymple Vivian, Henry Hussey's first wife who died

25th Feb. 1848. The figure stands on a pedestal bearing details in Latin of the birth, marriage and death of Jessie. As John Newman remarks, the figure seems 'oddly out of place in a Gothic shrine'. On the window sill of the second window is a small display case containing offertory bags made from the wedding dress of Jessie Vivian.

To the right of this window is a brass tablet to the memory of Gerald William Vivian, only brother of H.W. Vivian, who served in the Royal Navy from 1882-1921 and during the Great War commanded H.M.SS. *Europa*, *Patia*, *Liverpool* and *Roxburgh* in the Adriatic, North Sea and Atlantic Ocean on escort duty, d. 14th Aug. 1921.

In the west wall of the chapel, left of the entry doors (facing west) are two tablets, one commemorating Augusta Emily, 2nd daughter of the 3rd Earl of Dunraven, and wife of Arthur Pendarves Vivian (3rd son of John Henry Vivian), d. 11th Feb. 1877; the other Henry Wyndham Vivian of Glanafon, Port Talbot, eldest son of Arthur Pendarves and Lady Augusta Vivian, d. 17th Nov. 1901.

To the right of the entrance doors (facing west) is an elaborately carved niche shrine in the style of the canopies which contains a brass memorial to Caroline Elizabeth, second wife of Henry Hussey Vivian, d. 5th Jan. 1868.

The whole of the chapel floor is tiled and John Newman thinks that this pavement with its ornament of initials and armorial glass may be by Thomas Willament, who began his career as a painter of heraldic windows and latterly became stained glass artist to Queen Victoria and made an extensive series of windows for St. George's chapel, Windsor.

The Revd. Garfield James who introduced the aumbry for the Blessed Sacrament in the chapel in 1965, hoped that it would become a suitable place for private prayer and frequently celebrated the Wednesday morning eucharist there. During the extension of the chancel in 1928-29 a number of couples were married in the Vivian chapel, among them a future churchwarden and his wife, Mr. & Mrs. W. Hunt, the parents of Canon E.T. Hunt, former vicar of Christ Church.

The stained glass and heraldic devices in the chapel are dealt with in the next chapter.

Below the chapel lies the family vault with access down steps from outside. It contains the coffined remains of: Jessie Dalrymple Vivian, Henry Hussey Vivian, Caroline Elizabeth Vivian, Henry Wyndham Vivian, Augusta Emily Vivian, Henry Hussey Vivian (1st son of 1st Baron) by Averil, John Henry Vivian, Sarah Vivian, Richard Glynn Vivian, and Averil Vivian, Baroness Swansea.

Theft and Vandalism

Theft and vandalism have always been a problem for churches but such acts have occurred with increasing frequency in the second half of the twentieth century. In May 1960 the alms boxes were rifled of their contents and in July 1972 the choir vestry was broken into and a fire started. The oak robe cupboards were burned out and most of the choir robes destroyed or damaged, together with the choir and organ music. The Revd. Garfield James remarked in the magazine on 'the loss of simple trust which enabled us to keep our parish church open throughout every day . . . the church will now be locked for large parts of the day'. In July 1977 two windows on the north side were damaged and doors and windows sprayed with graffiti. From January 1978 a rota of vigilantes operated which allowed the church to be opened in the afternoons. Yet in the same month the vestry was again broken into, two fine oak doors smashed and a safe opened. The thief or thieves got away with £40-£50. In April 1978 the magazine reported damage by vandals to the window commemorating the life of St. Paul and forcible entry of the clergy vestry and theft of money from one of the safes. The 1980s appear to have been relatively free from incidents but in October 1993 there were further acts of theft and damage to the fabric which led to the installation of polycarbonate guard panels to the lower windows. One would have thought that the opening of the church centre with a more continuous presence of people within the church grounds would have put a stop to such acts but incidents continued and it was thought necessary in May 1998 to put polycarbonate guards over the high level stained glass windows which are vulnerable from the flat roof of the vestry. It is to be hoped that the new security devices which have been put in place will put an end to this problem.

The Church Plate

A note on the early plate

The theological and ecclesiological views of Woodyer, the architect of St. Paul's, influenced its layout, its architecture and the style of its early stained glass. Since Woodyer is also said to have taken a hand in the design of the binding of the early prayer and hymn books used at the church, it is reasonable to assume that this influence extended too to the style of church plate given to the church by early donors. Woodyer must have been a regular visitor to Sketty in the early 1850s, for in addition to the church, he designed the school (completed in 1853), and enlarged and remodel-

St. Paul's from south-east, *c.*1900
(City and County of Swansea Library Service)

St. Paul's Chancel
(J. Beynon)

Mosaics by Antonio Salviati

(J. Beynon)

East Window

(J. Beynon)

Vivian Chapel
Commemorative Windows
(J. Beynon)

St. Paul's Lectern
(J. Beynon)

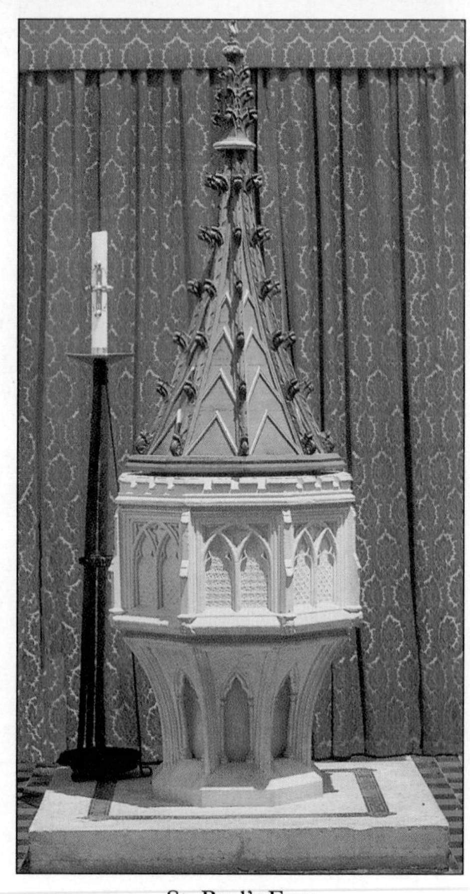

St. Paul's Font
(J. Beynon)

'St. Paul' Window
(J. Beynon)

'St. Paul' Window
(J. Beynon)

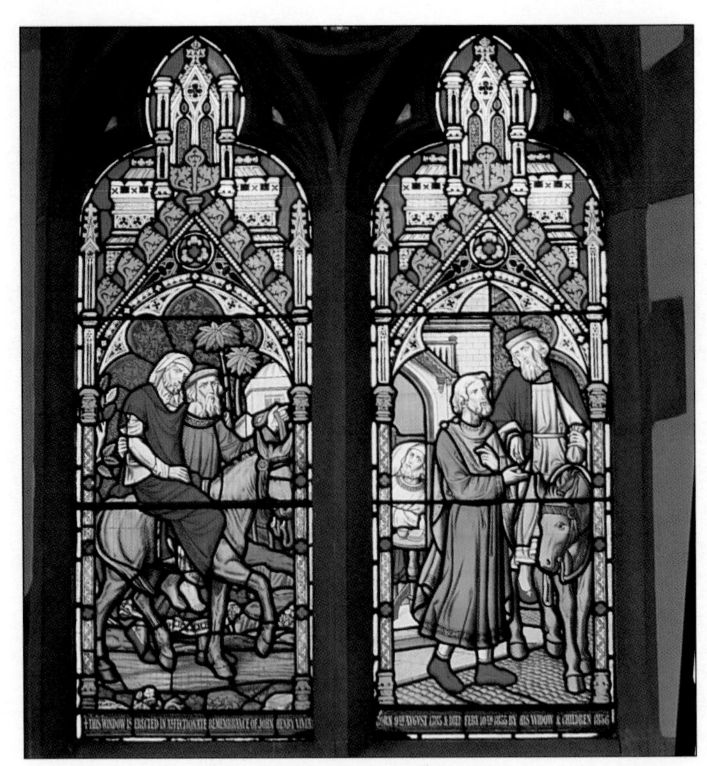

Good Samaritan Window

(J. Beynon)

Faith, Hope and Charity Window

(J. Beynon)

All Souls, Carnglas

(P. J. Gwynn)

Holy Trinity Church, Sketty Park

(A. Knight)

Ven. I. R. Luther Thomas
(J. Beynon)

Ven. R. J. Williams
(St. Paul's Church Archives/West Glamorgan Record Office)

Canon A. J. Knight, present Vicar

led in Gothic style the eighteenth century villa called Parc Wern (now Parc Beck Nurses' Home) where Henry Hussey lived until the death of his mother at Singleton in 1868. This return to the style of the Middle Ages can be seen in the earliest plate given to the church by the Eden family. The chalice and paten of silver gilt bearing the hall marks of 1850 with the maker's mark IK. for John Keith are of medieval design. The chalice (No. 1) is said to follow the design of one at Trinity College, Oxford, dated 1527. Around the bowl is engraved the legend + Calicem. salutaris accipiam. et. nomen dni invocabo: I will receive the cup of salvation and call upon the name of the Lord. At the foot is a crucifix and the shortened text: Calicem salutaris accipiam. with conventional leaf between each word. Beneath the foot is the inscription to the donor, Revd. John Eden, 1850. The stem is hexagonal and embellished with cable ornament and open tracery work, each of the six facets on the knop containing a rose. The base of the stem is decorated with open embattled work. Around the rim of the paten (No. 2) is engraved Agnus Dei qui tollis peccata mundi, miserere nobis (Lamb of God, who takes away the sins of the world, have mercy on us) and underneath, the inscription to the donor, Mrs. Frances Eden 1850. In the centre of the paten is a sexfoil depression in the middle of which is an enamelled agnus and flag. Mr. Charles and Mrs. Frances Eden, friends of J.H. Vivian, lived at the Bryn and were parents of the Revd. J.P. Eden. There is a similarly designed paten presented by Mrs. Frances Eden, 1850 (No. 3) which has around its rim the inscription Per crucem et passionem tuam libera nos Domine (By Thy cross and passion deliver us O Lord) and in the centre of the depression the sacred monogram IHC (the first letters of the Greek spelling of Jesus).

The alms basin (No. 4) in silver gilt by John Keith also bears the hall mark of 1850 and around the rim the legend + Benedic anima mea domino et noli oblivisci omnes retributiones eius (Bless the Lord O my soul and forget not all his benefits). The centre is decorated in repoussé with the scene of the Magi presenting gifts to the Holy Child. It was presented by Miss Mary Webber in 1850. The family had a close connection with St. Paul's in its early days and the earliest brass memorial tablet in the church, near the pulpit steps, records the death of Francis Gerald Webber, second son of the late Captain Arthur Webber, 47 Regiment, on 19th October 1853 aged twenty-three.

The chalice and paten presented by John Henry and Sarah Vivian in 1855 (Nos. 5 and 6) are of similar design to those of 1-3 but not quite as ornate. The chalice has the same inscription as no. 1 around its bowl and the paten the same inscription as that on no. 3 with the sacred monogram in the centre. To the year 1855 also belongs the elegant silver gilt medieval style flagon (No. 7) by the same maker John Keith. Around the bowl is inscribed Gloria in Excelsis Deo' and beneath 'The gift of Robert and Marianna Lindsay'.

Richard Glynn Vivian, despite his reputation as a ne'er do well, was a generous benefactor to the church. The silver gilt alms dish (No. 8) with French repoussé work was presented by him in 1896. It bears the marks H.D. linked with three fleurs-de-lis and is decorated with fruit, foliage and a scene representing the sacrifice of Isaac. The ewer or jug shaped flagon (No. 9) is decorated with French repoussé work representing Our Lord's Baptism and Ascension and was presented to the church by Richard Glynn Vivian in the same year. J.T. Evans in his *Church plate of Gowerland* (1921) records other gifts by him: a brass altar cross, six altar vases and two standard lights, inscribed 'Ex tenebra lux. Bought by R. Glynn Vivian at Rouen 1898'. The gas-lit standard lights stood during his lifetime at each side of the altar. J.T. Evans also lists as belonging to St. Paul's a copper font ewer with the inscription: 'John Henry & Sarah Vivian to St. Paul's, Sketty'. This has recently been recovered from the vicarage and now stands with another copper ewer near the font.

Schedule of Church Plate

List of chalices, patens, flagons, alms dishes, basons etc.

The descriptions of the church plate which follow reproduce those in the *Parish inventory: schedule of church plate.* The order of the entries has been re-arranged, however, to bring together related items and to produce a chronological order as far as possible. The items have been renumbered from 1 to 28 but the inventory numbers have been added for ease of reference to the original descriptions which reproduce the hall marks and photographs of each item.

1. Chalice – silver gilt
   Height – 9", bowl 4⅝", foot – 5½", weight 18oz. 1dwt
   Inscription – Presented to St. Paul's Church Sketty by the Rev. John Eden. 1850. (36)

2. Paten in silver gilt with enamel centre
   Diameter 7", weight – 6oz 6dwt
   Inscription – Presented to St. Paul's Church, Sketty by Mrs. Frances Eden. 1850. (40)

3. Paten in silver gilt with enamel centre
   Diameter 7", weight – 6 oz 6dwt
   Inscription – Presented to St. Paul's Church, Sketty by Mrs. Frances Eden. 1850. (42)

4. Alms basin in silver gilt
   Diameter 10½", weight – 14 oz 2dwt
   Inscription – Presented to St. Paul's Church, Sketty by Miss Mary Webber. 1850. (49)

5. Chalice – silver gilt
   Height – 9", bowl -4⅝", foot – 5½", weight 19 oz 9dwt
   Inscription – The gift of John Henry and Sarah Vivian. 1855. (35)

6. Paten in silver gilt with enamel centre
   Diameter 7", weight – 6 oz 15dwt
   Inscription – The gift of John Henry and Sarah Vivian. 1855. (41)

7. Flagon in silver gilt
   Height – 12", diameter of base 4⅝", weight – 30 oz 16dwt
   Inscription – the gift of Robert and Marianne Lindsay. 1855. (51)

8. Alms basin in silver gilt with French repoussé work.
   Diameter of top 12¾". Base – 7", weight 27 oz 19dwt
   Inscription – Presented to St. Paul's Church, Sketty by R. Glynn Vivian, Easter 1896. (50.1)

9. Ewer in silver gilt with French repoussé work
   Height 11", diameter at top 4¾", base 5", weight 23 oz 8dwt
   Inscription – Presented to St. Paul's Church, Sketty by R. Glynn Vivian, Easter 1896. (50.2)

10. Silver chalice and paten for sick communion in wooden box.
    Inscription – St. Paul's Church, Sketty
    Inscription on paten – To be used to the Glory of God and in Loving Memory of 2nd Lieut. Frederick W. Gibbon 1st Northumberland Fusiliers. Killed in Action at Le Sars

France 25th Aug. 1918. Given by his sister Mrs. Crouch, Pasadena, Sketty. (57)

11. Credence paten in silver
Diameter 7", weight 12 oz.
Inscription – A thank offering Edith Maria Schleswick, 1931. (44)

12. Paten in silver
Diameter 7½", weight 10 oz 8dwt
Inscription – Presented to St. Paul's Church, Sketty, by Mrs. Tunbridge in memory of her sister Mrs. Polybank 1935. (43)

13. Two flagons in silver
Each inscribed – In memory of Robert Evans 1947-1966. (53)

14. Chalice and paten
Paten – 5" diameter
Chalice – bowl – 3½", foot 3¼", height 5"
Inscription – In Memory of Denise Margery Maliphant Davies 1921-1969. (38)

15. Wafer box in silver set on four small round feet
4⅛" x 2" x 1½". Cross on lid.
Inscription – In loving memory of our mother MARY ISOBEL MORRIS 1902-1992. (48)

16. Chalice used for Reserved Sacrament kept in aumbry
Silver gilt
Bowl 2¼", height 5"
Inscription – D.B.W. The gift of his wife. (46)

17. Old English ciborium silver and gilt interior
7½" high
A gift from St. Paul's Altar Flower Guild. 1995. (58)

18. Ciborium in silver
Height with cover 8⅝", weight with cover – 14 oz
Given in memory of Miss Annie Jeanetta Russell by her brothers and sisters. (45)

19. Baptismal shell in silver
    In memory of A.V. Grove. (52)

20. Chalice – silver
    Bowl 3½", foot 4¼", height 6½", weight 10 oz 8dwt (37)

21. Chalice and paten
    Paten – 5" diameter
    Chalice – bowl 3", foot 3¼" height 5½"
    Cross stamped on chalice and paten. (39)

22. Wafer box in silver type
    6¾" x 4½" x 2". I.H.S. in blue on lid
    The gift of an anonymous donor. (47)

23. 1 small silver paten
    3¼" diameter. (54.1)

24. 1 small jug silver type
    Height 2¼", base 1¾" diameter. (54.2)

25. Silver gilt pyx – bottle missing. (54.3)

26. Two small sick communion sets
    Comprising 2 chalices, 2 wafer boxes, 1 glass bottle and paten. (55)

27. 1 silver stoppered carafe for Reserved Sacrament kept in aumbry. (56)

28. Black wooden box 4½" x 5½" x 9", sick communion set
    2 4½" cruets with silver plated stoppers
    1 chalice 3" high, 2" diameter bowl
    1 pyx 1¾" diameter silver-plated
    1 spoon 4¼" long silver with gilt bowl
    1 paten 3½" diameter silver plated. (59)

CHAPTER 6

The Stained Glass Windows and Decorative Art

by

MAURICE BROADY

Stained glass is so closely related to the building in which it is erected that it has justly been described as 'an architectural art'. A number of technical innovations – the pointed arch, the ribbed vault and the flying buttress – made it possible to build walls that were much thinner than those of Byzantine or Saxon buildings. This facilitated the use of windows as part of the structure of a church and, as this 'Gothic' style swept rapidly through western Europe in the early Middle Ages, it encouraged the use of the stained glass which Abbot Suger introduced in the newly-consecrated Abbey of Saint-Denis in Paris in 1144. Beginning with simple, one-light lancets, the tracery became increasingly elaborate and through into the sixteenth century much larger windows were steadily introduced which made use of more ornate, curvilinear, and rectilinear tracery.

Glazing served not only to keep out the cold and the rain. Stained glass was also intended to enhance the interior of cathedrals and churches with light and colour and thus to create an atmosphere that would be particularly conducive to Christian worship. It could also present Biblical scenes and characters pictorially and so help an illiterate laity to a better understanding of their faith. But above all, stained glass had to enhance the fabric within which it was erected. As Henry Holiday, one of the leading glass artists of the late nineteenth century put it: 'whatever beauty the details of . . . (stained glass) work may possess, it will fail in its first duty if it fights the architectural forms which it should adorn'.

From the early years of the sixteenth century, however, the Protestant fear of Catholicism and abhorrence of what was regarded as Popish idolatry led to a wide-spread hostility to the pictorial representation of Biblical subjects. This, together with the desecration of churches during the Cromwellian Commonwealth and the gross neglect of Anglican churches that continued into the eighteenth century, contributed to the virtual neglect of stained glass that lasted for some three hundred years. The revival of the medium in the eighteenth century at first produced stained glass that was mainly secular and which often entailed copying paintings onto rectangular pieces of glass, ignoring the role which lead-lines had traditionally played in design and using enamel paint which masked the light which, with medieval stained glass, had permeated the buildings in which it was erected.

During the eighteenth century, with the beginning of the Romantic movement, an interest in medieval antiquities began to develop. This growing interest in the Middle Ages subsequently informed the two major reform movements which so profoundly affected the Church of England during the nineteenth century. The Oxford Movement, on the one hand, was primarily concerned with questions of authority within the Church, while the Cambridge Camden Society (founded in 1839), and the self-styled 'Ecclesiologists', were committed to propagating ideas about the proper form of ritual and decoration in the Church of England. Like the Oxford Movement, the Ecclesiologists looked back to the early Middle Ages for inspiration. They followed Augustus Pugin (1812-1852) in regarding the Gothic style of the turn of the fourteenth century as the kind of church architecture that was most appropriate for Christian worship and, in what became known as 'the Gothic Revival', an active interest in medieval stained glass was revived and encouraged. Nowhere was this interest more enthusiastically expressed than by John Mason Neale, the divine, hymn-writer and leading supporter of the Revival, who wrote in 1843: 'A church is not as it should be till *every* window is filled with stained glass, till every inch of floor is covered with encaustic tiles . . . For it may safely be asserted that ancient churches in general were so adorned'.

The Ecclesiologists' zealous campaign to encourage churches to emulate medieval examples was conducted with such stern resolve that, by the middle of the nineteenth century, it had come to be generally accepted that churches should be built in the Gothic style – and not only churches, but even Nonconformist chapels and secular buildings, such as town halls, too. This conviction gained even greater sway as the population of England and Wales grew between 1831 and 1901 from thirteen to more than twenty million and as the number of churches steadily increased. Over 5,000 Anglican churches and chapels were erected during that period, an increase of nearly 50 per cent, while 1,376 Roman Catholic churches were built between 1840 and 1913.

These developments brought about a high and continuing demand for stained glass windows, especially from the Anglican and Roman Catholic communions, so that Martin Harrison's statement is hardly surprising that 'a conservative estimate of the number of stained glass windows supplied in the Victorian period to churches in England and Wales alone would be in the region of 80,000'. This demand was met in part by 'trade firms' working primarily for profit, which turned out stained glass of poor quality, often ordered from pattern-books. However, many new churches were being designed by distinguished architects, many of whom had High Church leanings, and their aesthetic and religious commitment led them to encourage artists of their persuasion to set up stained glass studios in order to design windows of high quality which could be erected in their churches.

Among these architects, two – George Gilbert Scott (1811-78) and William Butterfield (1814-1900) – were contemporaries of Pugin, and they were particularly influential among the slightly younger generation who were only in their twenties when Pugin died, at the age of forty, in 1852. All of them were Anglo-Catholics and they were all particularly interested in stained glass. Indeed, as Martin Harrison further notes, it was 'the close supervision of interiors as well as external colour and design which these leading architects would demand', together with 'the intense involvement in church decoration of a vast body of wealthy patrons, clergymen and ecclesiastics of all kinds', which influenced the development of stained glass during the High Victorian era. One of these younger architects who were committed to the Gothic Revival was Henry Woodyer (1818-96). He had been a pupil in Butterfield's office and by 1847 he had clearly demonstrated his commitment to the ideas of Pugin and the Ecclesiologists in the design of his first major commission for the parish church at Highnam in Gloucestershire. John Henry Vivian (1785-1855), the founder of the Vivian dynasty in Swansea, quickly retained him to build St. Paul's, which was consecrated three years later, in 1850.

Stained Glass and Other Memorials

The prime function of a church is to commemorate in the Eucharist Christ's sacrifice on the Cross, His Resurrection and His role in man's salvation. The parish church thus becomes the natural place in which the community of church-people commemorates its own history, and especially the lives of those who have contributed to its development. Over the centuries, commemoration has taken various forms. From the late thirteenth down to the fifteenth century people were commemorated in monumental brasses, while donors also begin to be found in stained glass windows from the late thirteenth century. In the sixteenth century, however, fostered no doubt by the Renaissance interest in classical antiquity, and at a time when stained glass was anathematized as idolatrous, memorials were more likely to take the form of stone monuments and plaques. The

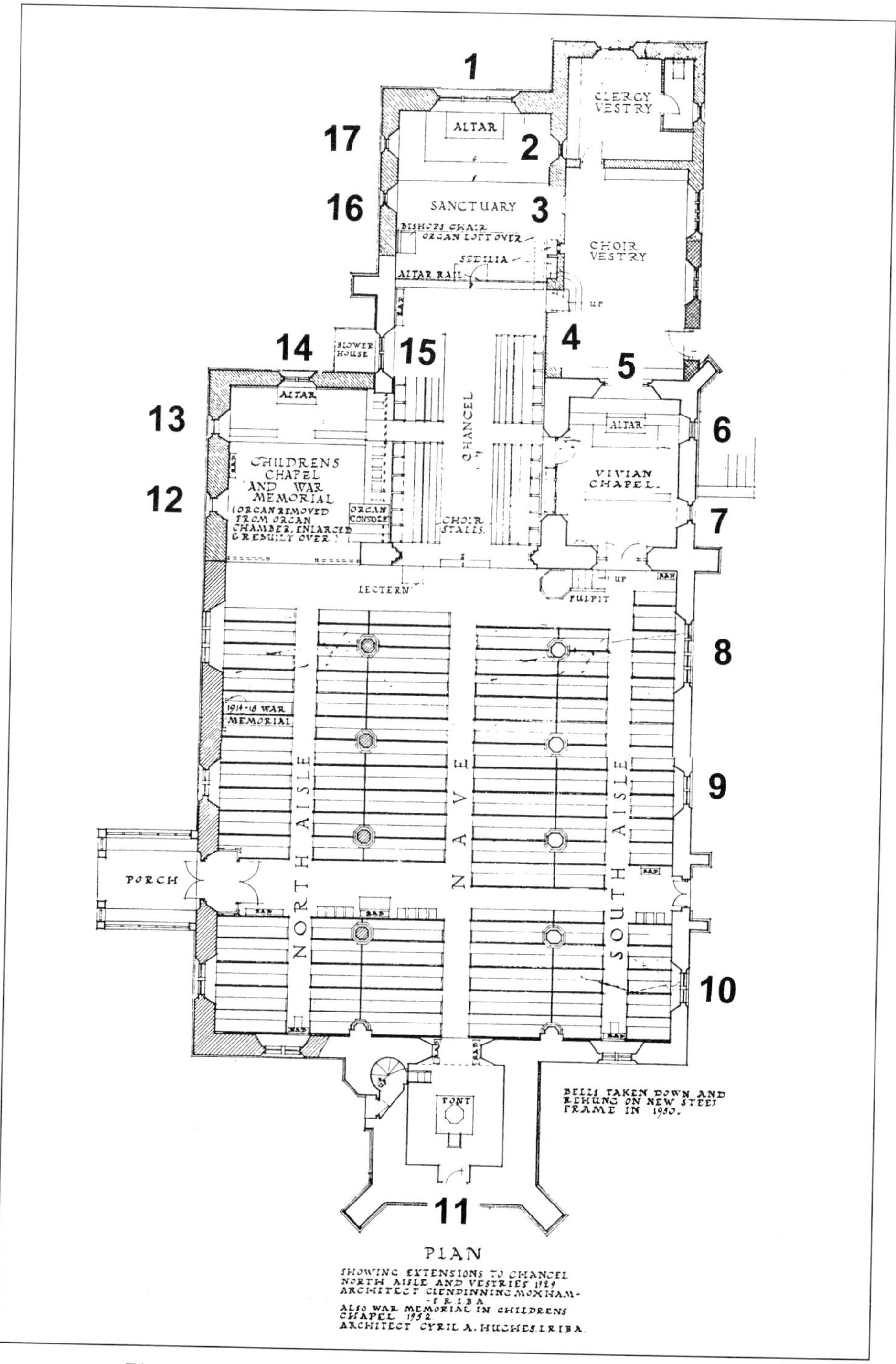

Plan of St. Paul's, 1952 (with numbered stained glass windows)
(St. Paul's Church Archives/West Glamorgan Record Office)

Gothic Revival in turn repudiated memorial sculpture, making stained glass fashionable again so that, after about 1840, obituary windows were in growing demand. In designing memorial windows to be erected in a church, it was usually necessary to refer to some Biblical scene, event or personage.

St. Paul's itself was built specifically to commemorate Jessie (1825-48), the wife of Henry Hussey Vivian (1821-94), John Henry's eldest son, who had died in childbirth after a marriage of barely a year's duration. The St. Paul's windows fall into three phases. Almost all of the eight windows that were erected between the consecration of the church in 1850 and the First World War commemorate members of the Vivian family. That there were other church members who were sufficiently well-off to have been able to pay for a stained glass window can hardly be doubted. But the fact that no donors other than the Vivians or their kin by marriage actually did so confirms the view that St. Paul's was regarded as the Vivians' church, the locus of the family cult which, like a royal chapel, could not be appropriated for anyone else's memorials. However, when the Vivians finally sold Singleton Abbey in 1919, a second phase began in which members of the Glasbrook family enlarged the church and erected five windows in the chancel. Their wealth and status, though by no means as great as the Vivians', had been built upon the family's interests in coal and timber. The original east window was replaced by one dedicated to John Glasbrook, who died in 1923, and four more windows were donated in 1939. In the third phase, since the Second World War, only three windows have been erected, which commemorate two local men of much lower status than the Glasbrooks.

In writing about these windows, we are hampered by the lack of contemporary documents, such as parish magazines. It is therefore often difficult to establish the precise date when, and the circumstances in which a particular window was erected. It is equally difficult to establish the firm, and still harder, the designer who made the window. The east window and the three post-war windows all show the firm's mark or name. But for the rest, attributions have had to be made as reliably as possible on stylistic grounds. We are indebted to Peter Cormack of the William Morris Gallery, Walthamstow, and to Martin Harrison for their assistance in this matter.

The Vivian Era: First Phase 1848-1860

The earliest windows in the church (see numbered plan on p. 89) are those in the baptistery (No. 11), the St. Paul window in the south nave (No. 8), the three in the Vivian chapel (Nos. 5, 6 and 7) and the Good Samaritan window (No. 15) in the chancel.

Since St. Paul's was designed to include a small Vivian mausoleum, the three windows in the Vivian chapel were most likely erected when the church was consecrated in 1850. Although the architect, Henry Woodyer, employed John Hardman of Birmingham as his glazier throughout his career, these windows were most probably designed by Thomas Willament (1785-1871). One of the leading glass artists working before the Gothic Revival, he was, in Harrison's opinion, 'the finest artist . . . practising in the early 1840s'. He was appointed heraldic artist to King George IV and subsequently artist in stained glass to Queen Victoria. Although these windows are not included in the list of Willament's work in the British Library (which, in any case, is said to be incomplete), he had previously been retained by John Vivian to design an armorial window for his original Swansea house, Marino, which he took over in 1817, and in 1828 and then in 1854 armorial windows for Singleton Abbey.

Of the Vivian chapel windows, only the one above the altar (No. 5) has a specifically religious connotation. In each of its six trefoils there is an attractive vine motif with simple white leaves, yellow tendrils and bunches of green grapes, which bespeaks Christ's saying 'I am the True Vine'.

The two lancet windows on the south wall of the chapel commemorate John Henry Vivian and his wife Sarah (No. 6) and Henry Hussey Vivian and his first and second wives, Jessie Dalrymple Goddard of Swindon and Caroline Elizabeth Cholmeley of Easton Hall, Grantham (No. 7). Since this lancet was presumably erected shortly after the death of Hussey's first wife in 1848, it was probably changed to include the heraldic reference to the family of his second wife, whom he did not marry until 1853.

These windows are entirely secular, designed with heraldry, monograms and quarries in a manner that would have been familiar to Willament in his earlier years, before the Gothic Revival made the depiction of Biblical motifs once more acceptable. They are alike in displaying a coat of arms in the trefoil and in placing two monograms, using an eclectic variant of Gothic lettering, in ornate wreaths above and below a shield within a leafy cartouche. The left-hand light (No. 6) shows the Vivian arms in the trefoil and, in the cartouche, the Vivian shield impaled with the silver stag of his wife's family, the Jones' of the Priory, Reigate. Sarah Jones was descended from a landed family from St. Asaph, one member of which had moved to London, probably as a lawyer, about 1761. In the wreaths are the initials of John Henry and Sarah Vivian. The right-hand light (No. 7) has the arms of Henry Hussey Vivian, differenced with the white label in the chief to indicate his status as John Henry's eldest son. In the wreaths, his initials are placed above, together with those of Jessie Dalrymple and below, with those of his second wife, Caroline Elizabeth. The shield in the centre similarly shows Henry Hussey's shield impaled with those of his wives' families, Goddard above and Cholmeley below.

Six shields are also painted on the front of one of the imitation tombs in the Vivian chapel, which John Henry Vivian had copied from the family church in Truro and installed here in memory of his parents and brothers. Read from left to right, they are the shields of the Vivians of Truro; of John Vivian impaled with what is presumably the shield of his wife, Betsy Cranch (though this cannot be authenticated); of Sir Charles Crespigny Vivian, who was appointed Baron Vivian in 1841, with his shield showing the 'augmentation' of two medals and a wreath which adorn the chief, now also 'embattled', in recognition of his valour during the Peninsula wars and at Waterloo; the Vivians of Singleton; Vivian impaled with Jones for John Henry Vivian; and finally the shield of John Vivian's third son, Thomas, distinguished by the cadency mark of a molet on the blue chevron.

The chapel also contains a white marble statue of an angel which was erected in memory of Jessie Dalrymple Vivian, whose tragic and early death in 1848, following the birth of her son, led to the building of St. Paul's. It stands over a small child which is sitting at its feet, holding a rose, the traditional symbol of love. A snake, symbolising evil, slithers away from the child. It is by the distinguished Italian sculptor Pietro Tenerani (1789-1869) in a classical style which, as John Newman has justly commented, is 'oddly out of place in this Gothic shrine'. The tiles which carry a pattern of interlaced Vs for Vivian, may be by Thomas Willament, who also designed the three windows in the chapel. High up on the arch of the chapel is a lozenge-shaped hatchment or funeral escutcheon of John Henry Vivian, which indicates that he was survived by his wife, Sarah.

The baptistery window in the tower (No. 11) was probably erected at the Vivians' expense when the church was built and was most likely designed by William Warrington (1796-1869) who also designed the original east window. The location of the font at the west end of the church, opposite to the altar where the Holy Eucharist, the prime sacrament in the church's liturgy, is celebrated, symbolises the child's reception into the Church by baptism. One of the first generation of stained glass designers to be associated with the Gothic Revival, Warrington had been trained in Thomas Willament's studio and, before setting up his own firm, he had been retained by Pugin himself to make the important windows in St. Mary's College, Oscott, the Roman Catholic college, in 1838.

A two-light window with a quatrefoil above, predominantly red and blue, its subject is stated on a long scroll held by an angel in the quatrefoil with the text 'Suffer the little children to come unto me' (Matthew

19:14; Mark 10:14 and Luke 10:14). It shows, left, Christ being baptised by John the Baptist with a white dove, representing the Holy Spirit, radiating three rays of light; and right, a seated Christ holding up His hand in blessing, among three children with curiously troubled faces and a saint with a red halo, who may be St. Nicholas of Myra, the patron saint of children.

These scenes are placed under canopies, occupying half the height of each light, which rest upon shafting and which incorporate large crockets and white brick-work. This idiom originated in the early fourteenth century, when glaziers imitated the architectural vocabulary of the mason to provide a frame for the figures which they depicted. The glaziers of the Gothic Revival sought to follow this medieval pattern by adopting these canopies and the two-dimensional design, and – in the Christ with the children light – by placing the figures on black and white tiling. They also made use of a decorated pillar as a simple, stylised way of showing that the events, such as Christ with the children, take place indoors.

The St. Paul window (No. 8) in the south wall of the nave was also one of the first to have been erected. Lacking documentary evidence, any assessment of its provenance can only claim to be plausible speculation. Since it is placed above a brass plaque memorialising William Jones Loyd MA JP DL of Langleybury, Hertfordshire (1821-1885), it appears to be an obituary window, but this is not the case. The Loyds were a Carmarthenshire family, one of whose sons had moved to London as a banker, probably at the turn of the eighteenth century. William's coat of arms in the middle light of the tracery shows the Jones Loyd shield impaled with Vivian, since he married John Henry's second daughter, Caroline Gertrude.

Their marriage took place in June 1848, barely four months after Henry Hussey's first wife, Jessie, had died. William Jones Loyd was already closely associated with the Vivian family at this time. He and Hussey Vivian had been contemporaries both at Eton and at Trinity College, Cambridge, both were aged twenty-seven and both were actively rising in their family businesses of banking and copper-smelting. So when John Henry and Hussey resolved to erect a church as a memorial to Jessie, it is highly probable that William Jones Loyd, torn between sympathy for his friend's bereavement and happiness at his own impending marriage, should have donated a window to the new church. I also surmise that he requested Henry Woodyer to design a special frame for this window since it is the largest window, apart from the east window, in the church and the only one with four lights and such complicated tracery.

When, in 1863, William Jones Loyd decided to follow Henry Hussey's lead by building a church at Langleybury, near Watford, as a memorial to his parents, he too retained Woodyer as his architect and also dedicated the church to St. Paul. Three Langleybury windows were donated by members of the Vivian family. The east window and three windows in the nave (two of which were given by Sir Hussey and Graham Vivian in 1866) are clearly by the same artist who designed the St. Paul window. While William Warrington has been suggested as the likely designer, they were in fact designed by the French firm of Gsell-Laurent. Jules-Gaspard Gsell (1814-1904) arrived in Paris from Switzerland in 1840 and, as an associate of Emile Laurent, eventually became the head of this firm.

Compared with the other windows that were erected in St. Paul's, Sketty in and about 1850, though the four scenes from the saint's life are placed on plinths and under canopies that hark back to the Gothic, the St. Paul window is worked in a much more painterly, three-dimensional and naturalistic idiom (St. Paul, for instance, is not given a halo), a style characteristic of the sixteenth century which was totally at variance with the 'true principles' of stained glass that Pugin had advocated.

This window is sharply divided between the pictorial scenes and the spacious and most unusual tracery. This tracery comprises three large, elongated quatrefoils, four trefoils and four smaller lights. The basic design is a motif of red roses, symbolising martyrdom, with white leaves and tendrils upon a ground of yellow stain with black hatching. The large quatrefoil in the centre shows the arms of Loyd impaled with Vivian, with the Loyd crest of a stag's head and the family's motto 'Non mihi sed patriae' – 'Not for me but for the country' – while, in the quatrefoil below, the interlaced letter L for Loyd is set upon a red ground. In the two adjacent quatrefoils there are red roundels containing, left, a Chi-Rho monogram (the first two letters of 'Christ' in Greek) and, right, a similar monogram with Alpha and Omega – the beginning and the end – beneath the bar. Finally, on scrolls above these roundels are the words 'CRUCIFERO PAX': 'to Him who bears the Cross, peace'.

Underneath the monogram, on a downward extension of the Chi-Rho sign, is a mysterious bird on a horizontal bar. The fact that a similar dove is also found in a Gsell-Laurent window in Langleybury church suggests that this is the artist's mark.

The main feature of this interesting window, however, are the four scenes from the life of St. Paul. Each scene is set upon traditional masonry plinths bearing small shields with the monogram 'SP' for St. Paul and bottony crosses and placed beneath unusual twin canopies, supported by simple shafting. On the plinths, the four episodes are indicated on scrolls in a kind of Lombardic lettering with the Latin words CONVERSIO

– Conversion; PRAEDICATIO – Preaching; JUDICIUM – Brought to Trial; and NAUFRAGIUM – Shipwreck. This unusual use of the Latin was presumably intended to indicate the seriousness of the subject. The first and last events take place out-of-doors, while the two central episodes are indoors.

In the conversion scene, Saul, accompanied by soldiers and a peasant, is shown vigorously reining in his startled horse as he looks up with an anguished expression to a ray of light bearing in Latin the question 'Saul, Saul, why persecutest thou me?' (Acts 9:4), emanating from a heavy cloud which hangs menacingly over the distant landscape.

The preaching scene rather belies the Biblical location of Paul's sermon on Mars Hill (Acts 17:22-3) since it is taking place inside a building with a tiled floor, classical arches and a seat also decorated in classical style. St. Paul stands, the Scripture in his hand and with his right hand raised to Heaven, as he preaches to a dozen men and women who have crowded in to hear him. On the wall between two arches are the words 'IGNOTO DEO' – 'To the unknown god' – the expression of a superstition which Paul had seen on an altar and against which he was preaching in Athens.

The judgement is also depicted as taking place in a similar hall – 'Herod's judgement hall'. St. Paul is shown, escorted by two centurions, standing before Felix, the Roman governor of Caesarea, who sits on a large chair with a tasselled canopy, thoughtfully stroking his beard. (Acts 24). (This light has painted on it a 'GG' mark with the year 1953, the significance of which it has not been possible to establish).

In the final scene, Paul is depicted on the island of Melita, where he had been shipwrecked when he was being taken to Rome to appeal to Caesar against his sentence. With an attractive view of the sea, sailing-ships on the shore, a landscape and billowing clouds behind him, St. Paul is found sitting at a wooden fire which the 'barbarous people' had lit for them. Two Roman centurions standing behind him, the one leaning upon a spear and the other holding a banner on which are the letters 'SPQR' (Senatus Populusque Romanus – the Senate and the Roman People), join four other spectators as they look with astonishment at a small viper that has fastened itself on to St. Paul's hand. But when he shook it off and suffered no harm, instead of regarding him as a murderer, the barbarians took him to be a god! (Acts 28:1-6).

The last window to be erected in the years immediately following the consecration of St. Paul's in 1850 is the Good Samaritan window (No. 15) on the north wall of the chancel. This window was dedicated to John Henry Vivian by his wife and their children and was erected in 1856. John Henry (1785-1855) was the member of the Vivian family who established the firm's operations in Swansea in the early years of the nineteenth century, residing in the house which became Singleton Abbey shortly after his marriage to Sarah Jones in 1817. The subject of the window, the Good Samaritan, while suitably Biblical, was also no doubt chosen to indicate his personal virtues as a good employer and local benefactor.

This window is attributed to the firm of William Wailes of Newcastle-upon-Tyne. Wailes, a grocer and tea-dealer with artistic inclinations, set up a stained glass studio in 1838 which, together with Hardman's in Birmingham, became the two largest studios outside London. A Gothic Revivalist, he was employed by Pugin and by William Butterfield and George Edmund Street, (1824-81) two of the leading Gothic Revival architects. Following precisely Pugin's precepts about the 'true principles' of glass-painting, which contrasted so sharply with the 'pictorial' style which Gsell-Laurent had adopted in designing the St. Paul window, Wailes's excellent design admirably illustrates what Pugin advocated: the restriction of a design to two-dimensions and the use of leading not only to incorporate the myriad pieces of glass in the medieval manner but also to act as an integral part of the design.

A singularly attractive, two-light window, it displays in the trefoil above it the arms of Vivian impaling Jones, with the crest above and the motto below. The crest is unusual. In the heraldic description it shows 'issuant from a bridge embattled and at each end a tower, a demi-hussar of the 18th regt. holding in his right hand a sabre and in his left a pennon flying to the sinister gules and inscribed in letters or 'Croix d'Orade', a reference to the location of the bridge which Richard Hussey Vivian took in the closing stages of the Peninsula War, an exploit for which, at the special desire of the Prince Regent, he took this singular crest.

Although the Good Samaritan is a fairly hackneyed subject, it is excellently handled, with skilful draftsmanship, carefully delineated faces, subtle choice of colours and deft diaper-work, all of which gives the window a most engaging freshness. It is treated in the fourteenth century manner. Both scenes are framed by ornate canopies, with yellow crockets and white cusps, borne on shafting. In the left-hand light, set against a diapered blue sky, a couple of palm trees and the hint of a Palestinian building, the Samaritan holds the traveller 'who had fallen among thieves' solicitously but firmly on his horse, which he is leading forward along a flowery path. The Samaritan has draped his own red cloak around the man, leaving him wearing only his pink under-garment. Both of them wear expressions of anxiety on their faces. In the other light, we look onto the cobbled court-yard of an inn where, through an arch, the traveller can be seen in bed, with a medicine bottle, a cup and a book on the table at his side. He is looking, still anxiously, to where the Samaritan, mounted now and wearing his red cloak again, is giving the inn-keeper money which he has taken from his yellow purse. (Luke 10: 30-36).

THE VIVIAN ERA: SECOND PHASE, 1861-1920

Once the Samaritan window had been erected in 1856, there was a gap of some twenty years before the next window was installed in St. Paul's. By the 1870s, most church windows were still being designed in a Gothic Revival style little different from that of the early years of the Revival and, as Harrison comments, most firms 'continued to offer a debased and dilute Gothic Revival style for many years'. Even into the 1870s, some large, and very many smaller firms 'were content to rework already exhausted themes in an unconvincing and uninspired manner'.

Inevitably an artistic reaction set in. In 1861, William Morris set up the firm of Morris, Marshall, Faulkner & Co. whose glass increasingly departed from the Revival idiom as it adopted softer and more sensitive colours and as Burne-Jones, who was the firm's leading designer, moved steadily under the influence of the Italian Renaissance. The Aesthetic Movement of the 1870s and 1880s, with an increasing interest in domestic design, was also a reaction against the *gravitas* and pietism of the Gothicists, arguing that art should be judged not by any ulterior moral, political or religious purpose but by purely aesthetic criteria: art for art's sake. Finally, growing out of Morris's initiative, the Arts and Crafts Movement was established in the 1880s with the intention of ensuring, through the close association between designers and craftsmen, working together in relationships akin to the idealised guilds of the Middle Ages, that the quality and beauty should be restored in manufactured goods which had been debased by industrialisation.

The Faith and Charity window (No. 9) reflects these changes. It is an obituary window. John Henry Vivian's third son, Arthur Pendarves (1834-1924) had married Lady Augusta Emily Wyndham-Quin, the second daughter of the 3rd Earl of Dunraven, in 1867. She died in 1877 at the age of thirty-eight, while in Cannes. The window is attributed to the firm of Clayton and Bell. The firm's two partners, John Richard Clayton (1827-1913) and Alfred Bell (1832-95), were young men in their twenties when they set up their partnership in 1855, in what might be described as the second generation of Victorian glass studios. Clayton had studied at the Royal Academy Schools while Bell came from an apprenticeship with the foremost Gothic Revival architect, Sir George Gilbert Scott (1811-78), and they started what became one of the most prolific of all glass studios until the First World War. They were employed by the architect G.E. Street (1824-81), who had also worked in Scott's office, and were associated with the firm of Heaton and Butler, who were of an age with Clayton and Bell and who had also set up a studio in London in 1855. This association succeeded in 'consistently producing stained glass which, though its roots were in the thirteenth century, showed considerable originality in both colour and design'. They could also claim to have trained many leading glass artists of the following generation, including Charles Eamer Kempe (1834-1907), John Burlison (1843-91) and Thomas Grylls (1845-1913), whose studios both produced stained glass for St. Paul's.

This is an allegorical window, the figures representing two of the three Christian virtues, Faith and Charity. Whilst they have a Biblical reference (1 Corinthians. 13-13), they were also probably chosen to epitomise Lady Augusta's own virtues, as had been done so fulsomely on eighteenth century stone memorials. The Christian imagery in the tracery shows a bright red cross, surmounted by a delicately ornamented crown, which symbolises Christ's majesty and His victory over death. From the crown there radiate rays of light, while Heaven is indicated by the yellow and white stars on a deep blue ground which decorate the smaller lights.

Faith is portrayed in profile as a simple but confident young woman, holding a pastoral staff in her hand. Her yellow hair curls attractively over her shoulder and she wears a blue dress with a white cloak with light, yellow decoration draped over her arm. Charity, as befits a mother, is a more matronly figure who is standing, a babe in her arms, with two children, drawn in a rather heavy manner, one holding her hand and carrying a small bouquet of meadow-flowers, the other clasping her voluminous skirts.

The style of the Aesthetic Movement can be clearly seen in the golden hair, the delicately painted flower motif on the off-white dress with its cool and soft tones and, above all, by the panels of brown, floral roundels above which is a design of green leaves and yellow fruits. These have replaced the rather hackneyed plinths and canopies, taken from medieval patterns, which can still be seen in the adjacent window (No. 10) as well as in much traditional design until well into the 1950s.

The next window to have been erected, showing The Good Shepherd and Christ with the children (No. 10), was given by her children in memory of Sarah Vivian, who died in 1886, outliving her husband, John Henry Vivian, by thirty-one years. It is attributed to the firm of Burlison and Grylls who had both trained in the Clayton and Bell studios. They had come under the influence of the architect George Frederick Bodley (1827-

1907) who, like his contemporary, Street, had been a pupil of Sir Gilbert Scott and who was also a leading figure in the Gothic Revival. Through his influence, they received a number of important commissions, and it was Bodley and his partner, Thomas Gardner, who encouraged them to set up a studio together in 1868.

Burlison and Grylls, like Kempe, continued to produce designs in the Gothic style. Their conservatism, doubtless insisted upon by the donors, led to their continuing use of the plinths, shafting and complex canopy-work which many other designers, like Morris, Burne-Jones and artists in the Arts and Crafts tradition, were beginning to dispense with. In this two-light window with tracery, the figures of the Good Shepherd, left, and Christ with children, right, are both framed in this way.

In the tracery, the main quatrefoil shows a red shield with a PX monogram within a yellow wreath, together with a vine motif which is continued into the side lights. These contain roundels with a fish and a peacock, Christian symbols for baptism and immortality. In the main lights, Christ the Good Shepherd is depicted as a fair-haired, rather naïve youth with a lamb over His shoulder and sheep behind him. He stands in a meadow holding a staff, against a green landscape with a wattle fence and under a stormy blue sky, dressed in a simple red dress, brown boots and with a clear, cruciform halo. In the other light, against a similar background, a more mature and bearded Christ stands in a simple white dress and red cloak, carrying a babe-in-arms and with His right hand stretched out to a woman who kneels before Him as she looks up, her yellow hair over her shoulder, to present to Christ a child who stands before her. Another woman in a blue cloak and white cowl stands with her husband, a babe-in-arms and two other children beside her.

The last window to have been erected by the Vivians (No. 14) is the memorial to Henry Hussey Vivian (1821-94), John Henry's eldest son, who died in 1894 at the age of seventy-three, a year after becoming the first Baron Swansea in 1893. Also ascribed to Burlison and Grylls, it is stylistically very different from the previous window which this firm had designed barely ten years before. Since its subject is the conversion of St. Paul, it may well have been designed deliberately to resemble the St. Paul window of *c.*1850 (No. 8) in its pictorial and painterly style and its naturalistic idiom. While it retains very simple, narrow shafting as a border, this leads not to the conventional canopy-work but to an unusual black and white leaf motif, which shows how much less obligatory the Gothic Revival conventions had become by the last decade of the nineteenth century.

This is a two-light window with a trefoil. The trefoil, as in some of the other Vivian windows, contains the coat-of-arms of the recently elevated

Baron Swansea. This differs slightly from the earlier Vivian arms since it incorporates the red hand of Ulster on a silver shield (the sign of a baronet), is surmounted by a baron's coronet with four of its six silver balls visible, and has as the motto not 'Vivemus' but 'Vive anima Dei' – May the spirit of God live – which is a pun on the family's name.

Full-coloured, like all the earlier windows, it shows Christ in the left-hand light. Around Him, rays of light spread into the adjacent light, thus helping to unify the design across the mullion. He wears a jewelled white gown with a decorated yellow stole, also jewelled and tasselled, a red cloak with a green lining held at the neck with a clasp, and a blue halo with a yellow cross. He stands upon stylised purple clouds in a starry Heaven, raising His right hand to God the Father and holding out His left to Paul. (Acts 9:3ff.)

Paul, in the right-hand light, crouches on the grass with his right arm raised as if to shield his head. He has curly brown hair, a slight beard and moustache and he wears a blue gown decorated at neck and hem and a red cloak, both jewelled. Behind Paul, an armoured centurion restrains a finely caparisoned horse that is rearing up in fright, against a realistic depiction of the gates of Damascus under a deep blue sky. The text at the base of the window reads 'I have fought the good fight, I have finished my course, I have kept the Faith. Make him (*sic*) to be numbered with Thy Saints in Glory everlasting. Amen'. (2 Timothy 4: 7 and the Te Deum).

When John Aubrey Vivian died in 1898, Henry Hussey's half-brother, Ernest, who had succeeded him as the second Lord Swansea, commemorated John Aubrey not by erecting another window but by commissioning mosaics for each side of the east window. Given the very close relations between the Vivians and the Jones Loyds of Langleybury, these were probably designed and erected by the firm of Dr. Antonio Salviati of Venice, whose mosaics of St. Peter and St. Paul decorated the east wall of St. Paul's at Langleybury, and who was also designing mosaics for St. Paul's Cathedral.

The mosaics in St. Paul's Sketty depict, on the left, St. John the Evangelist and the Virgin Mary, holding the lilies which symbolise her purity. St. John holds the golden chalice from which the Emperor Diocletian, his persecutor, ordered him to drink the poisoned wine, which turned into a red dragon rising from the chalice when St. John took it up to obey. On the south side, there is King David with his harp and St. Cecilia, the patron-saint of music, with her portative organ. David and Cecilia presumably bespeak John Aubrey's interest in music, as a chorister in Penmaen parish church and as the donor of the organ at Penmaen when he died. The figures are placed upon simple plinths, beneath equally simple canopies and against a golden background. These mosaics complement the reredos, which is a stone relief of the Last Supper, probably also of Italian provenance, given by Sarah Vivian in 1878, which was erected at the same time as the marble which her husband had brought back from Italy.

Between the Wars

The death of Henry Hussey Vivian presaged the demise of the firm of Vivian and Sons. Scion of a Cornish copper-mining family, John Henry Vivian had come to Swansea in 1800 where he established the family's copper smelting business in 1809. By the 1830s, it had become one of the leading firms in the business. It continued to prosper when, a few years before John Henry's death in 1855, Henry Hussey (1821-1894) took over control of the firm, which he exercised for forty years until he died in 1894. By then, however, the Swansea copper industry was in decline. The Vivians were finding difficulty in recruiting workers and getting economical supplies of coal, problems which were aggravated by a lack of entrepreneurship which might have been able to seek out new markets and introduce more efficient technical processes. The selling of the Vivian's home at Singleton Abbey in 1919 marked the ending of their hegemony in Swansea, which finally ended in 1924, when Vivian and Sons was taken over by British Copper Manufacturers Ltd.

During the inter-war period, economic adversity in both urban and rural Wales meant that relatively few windows were commissioned. But there remained in Sketty many families of wealth and standing and it was the Glasbrooks who took over the Vivians' mantle as benefactors of St. Paul's. The Glasbrook dynasty had been founded by John Glasbrook (1815-1887) in the nineteenth century. Although they lacked the Vivians' aristocratic connections and their wealth and status were by no means as great as the Vivians', they had risen to economic eminence through the family's interests in coal and timber. When one of John Glasbrook's five sons, a leading Swansea businessman who was also called John (1849-1923), died in 1923, his wife Edith donated a new east window in his memory. East windows, being the most important in a church, were often donated by the industrial magnates or members of their families who endowed a local church, and erected when it was consecrated. The original window, depicting the Crucifixion and designed by William Warrington, had been presented by Sarah Vivian when the church was consecrated in 1850.

The new window (1) was made by C.E. Kempe & Co. of London, a well-known and prolific firm which was 'one of the most distinctive and successful in the later Victorian period'. Charles Eamer Kempe (1834-1907), like his contemporaries Morris and Burne-Jones, had intended to enter the Anglican ministry but, thwarted by a stammer, he had worked for two years in Clayton and Bell's studio when he came under the influence of the Gothic Revival architect, F.G. Bodley (1827-1907) who, like Alfred Bell, had trained in the office of Sir Gilbert Scott. Following fifteenth and early sixteenth century patterns, Kempe's designs met a very lucrative demand, producing an average of over sixty windows a year from 1868, when the studio was set up, to 1934 when it closed down. Their work remained extremely popular with High Church clergy, though it became increasingly stereotyped. As Harrison comments, 'figures were enmeshed in a mass of complex, overwrought canopy-work, landscape backgrounds became even more literal and pictorial, and the figures themselves were fussy and over-bejewelled, flashy and mannered in draftsmanship'. But at least there is no difficulty in attributing a Kempe window. For his mark, Kempe took from his family's arms an heraldic garb or sheaf. When he died in 1907, his nephew, Walter Tower (1873-1955) took over the firm, and he imposed a black tower upon the sheaf. This mark can be found in the bottom left-hand corner of this window.

Its design, presumably done by J.W. Lisle, Kempe's designer from 1907 till his death in 1927, is by no means as heavy and cluttered as Harrison's general comment would suggest. A three-light window with tracery, its subject is the Ascension. There are two bands of figures separated by quarries. This arrangement allows much more natural light to enter the church than was possible with the full-coloured windows which were erected previously and it also sets off the wide range of colours used in the rest of the window.

In the upper band high up in the middle light, Christ, vested in a simple white garment and a red cloak held at the neck with a clasp, stands bare-foot upon stylised grey clouds radiating light from His mandorla. At His feet, a long scroll gives the text 'This same Jesus shall so come in like manner as ye have seen Him go into Heaven' (Acts 1:11). In each of the flanking lights, three baby-faced cherubim are placed upon clouds from which emanate small rays of light. They wear highly decorated tunics and yellow haloes and have large wings of blue, red and green, together with the peacock feathers, a symbol of immortality, which are a characteristic of Kempe's designs. Two of them are playing instruments – a harp and a cornet – while the other four stand with their hands clasped or raised in praise.

This band is separated from the lower one by simply decorated quarries. Here, eleven disciples and the Virgin Mary, all with yellow haloes, stand or kneel in various postures of adoration and astonishment, dressed in blue, red and green and cloaks of different designs. In the middle of the central light, two ornately dressed angels, also with red and blue peacock-feathered wings, stand on either side of exquisitely painted greenery, on which can be seen the prints made by Christ's feet before His Ascension. These figures are placed in front of a landscape showing a river, medieval castles and a townscape which extends across all three lights. Although a traditional plinth serves as a base to the design, there is no canopy-work and the scenes are framed by borders showing a leaf motif, an IHC monogram and small bands of blue, red and green.

Increasingly the chancel became a memorial to the Glasbrooks. In 1928-9, they paid for the building of the vestry and the organ-chamber and, in 1939, John Glasbrook's son erected four more memorial windows in memory of his mother, Edith Amelia Glasbrook. If he had wished to commission designs similar to that of the east window, he would have discovered that Kempe's had gone out of business in 1934. So he turned to the firm of Burlison and Grylls which had been run by Thomas Henry Grylls (1873-1953) after his father's death in 1913. It seems likely that the designs for these four sanctuary windows were taken from nineteenth century cartoons.

Notwithstanding the discontinuity in design which this entailed, these windows have at least a thematic coherence with the east window, since they depict six Biblical scenes – the Resurrection and five episodes that followed Christ's Ascension. Since the lights on the north side of the sanctuary are rather larger than those on the south, they are able to contain two scenes, one above the other. The scenes move in sequence from the light at the western end of the north wall (No. 16) to the corresponding light on the south wall (No. 3). In all of them, the figure of Christ can be immediately recognised. He has a gentle face, yellow hair and beard, a white halo with a yellow rim and red decoration, and he wears a deep red cloak. His stigmata are clearly visible. The Gothic lettering communicates a sense of medieval seriousness to the depictions.

The first panel (No. 16) illustrates the text. 'He is risen, He is not here' (Mark 16:6). Against a heavy purple sky, with a view of a hill, a medieval castle, a cliff and trees, an angel stands on the stone slab of the sepulchre. He has white wings, and is dressed in white with a stole clasped at the neck and he wears a coronet fronted with a cross, (the Biblical text says 'a young man . . . clothed in a long white garment'). With his left hand pointing upwards, he is speaking to three haloed women, Mary Magdalene, Mary the mother of James and Salome, who had come to the sepulchre to anoint the dead Christ. One woman kneels, her hands clasped at her breast. She has yellow hair and wears a deep blue gown with, over it, a white and yellow mantle; an urn is beside her on the ground. The two other women are standing, similarly dressed, with one carrying another urn.

The second scene in the lower part of the light is also set against a purple sky with hills, stylised towers, a gate and a fence. Mary Magdalene, still with her urn at her side, raises her hands to Christ whom she had taken for a gardener. Loosely clad in a decorated red cloak which leaves his torso exposed, He is holding up His hand to say to her 'Touch me not' (John 20:18).

The third window (No. 17) shows two disciples walking along a path with attractive vegetation towards the village of Emmaus and with a naïve landscape of hills, rocks and trees in the background. They are talking together, as Jesus draws near. Even when He began expounding the Scriptures, they did not recognise Him and, when they eventually did so, He quickly vanished and the disciples said to one another 'Did not our heart burn within us, while he talked to us, and while he opened to us the Scripture' (Luke 24:32).

The text 'and . . . he was made known of them in breaking of bread' (Luke 24:35) is also illustrated in window No. 17. In a room with a tiled floor, on a table with a white cloth there is a jug, plates and a yellow chalice. A green drape with a yellow bejewelled band separates this room from a canopy and an arcade, through which a purple medieval building can be seen. On either side of the table sit the same two disciples, one in purple-red and the other in blue covered by a cloak, as Christ at the head of the table blesses a piece of bread.

Window No. 2 depicts the scene in John 20:19-29, in which Christ came into the room where His disciples had foregathered. Thomas was absent, since he doubted that Christ had been seen. Eight days later, however, he *was* persuaded when Christ appeared again and urged Thomas to thrust his hand to His side and to 'be not faithless, but believing', when Thomas cried out 'My Lord and my God'. The scene is placed on a plinth on which is black and white tiling and, alone among these scenes, beneath a canopy. Behind is a diapered brown drape, beyond which there are arches surmounted with an ornate canopy, through which a medieval townscape can be seen. Thomas, with yellow hair and a halo, and in a blue gown with a white mantle decorated at the hem, holds out his hand to touch Christ's chest, as two disciples look on.

The final window of this series (No. 3) illustrates the episode in John 21:15-16 in which Jesus appeared to His disciples for a third time and, after dining together, charged Simon Peter with the words 'Feed my lambs, feed my sheep'. Here, there is a stylised landscape with the typical purple sky, hills, crags and trees, and the Sea of Tiberias with a sailing-boat drawn up ashore. Christ stands with His right hand raised, pointing to Simon Peter in a blue dress, a yellow decorated gown and a yellow halo, who kneels, looking up to Christ, his hands clasped at his breast. Two disciples in green and purple-red gowns stand by, with sheep and lambs between them, their hands raised in adoration.

In the chancel there is also the bishop's chair with carvings of two kneeling angels and a mitre and the shield of the Diocese of Swansea and Brecon set on its elaborately carved back.

The Post-War Period

The choice of these four windows, with their insipid draftsmanship and a style that harks back to the nineteenth century, shows how conservative, or how uninformed was John Glasbrook's aesthetic judgement, which ignored, for example, the work of many artists in the Arts and Crafts tradition who could have offered more modern and more interesting designs. Since the Second World War, only three windows have been erected in St. Paul's and these, too, are merely competent and uninspired.

All three windows are by Gerald Smith (1883-1959) of St. John's Wood, London. Smith was born in 1883 and apprenticed to Edward Frampton (1846-1929) who had spent some time in the 1860s working in Clayton and Bell's studio, one of the more innovative firms of the Gothic tradition. In 1906, he joined the studio of A.K. Nicholson (1872-1937), which he ran until 1959 after Nicholson died in 1937. He designed Nicholson's memorial window in St. Sepulchre-without-Newgate in the City of London.

The small window on the south wall of the chancel (No. 4) was erected in 1954. It was dedicated by his wife to Lewis Edward Webber, the manager of a Swansea furniture store. Intended no doubt to epitomise her own felicitous family life, it depicts, against clear rectangular quarries, the Holy Family in a flower-garden with a stream, a wall, a tree that rises up to the head of the light and a distant view of hills and a castle. The Virgin Mary, in white with a blue cloak, sits sewing and the baby Jesus sits on the ground with arms outstretched, while Joseph, in a red gown, holds a plank.

The two lancet windows which were erected in the north wall of the children's chapel in 1956 were dedicated to Herbert Bassett, a Swansea hotelier, by his wife and son. Separated by an expanse of wall, they both have a main figure set against clear quarries with a smaller panel below it.

The use of clear glass shows an awareness that full-coloured windows cut out too much natural light. In a pamphlet on choosing stained glass published in the 1960s, Eric Milner-White, then the Dean of York, commented that the Victorians 'over-darkened the whole church . . . with hurt alike to its beauty, to the joy of its worship – and to expenditure on artificial lighting', and added the point 'that the very meaning of a window is to admit light'.

One of the windows (No. 12) shows St. David. A Welsh harp is in the head of the light, with a scroll bearing 'Saint David of Wales' and, lower down, a red Welsh dragon set upon green. St. David stands on a green bank on which daffodils grow. He wears a mitre as Bishop of Menevia, and he is vested for the administration of the Eucharist with a blue halo, a white under-garment with deep red decoration, a chasuble, pallium and a dalmatic decorated in black and white. He raises his hand in blessing and holds a pastoral staff which incorporates a Celtic cross, while the Dove of the Holy Spirit, against a white cross, radiates light. In the panel, the statement that the church was dedicated by Bishop Thirlwall in 1850 accompanies the depiction of the bishop with his crook, with St. Paul's in the background.

The twin window (No. 13) depicts the Archangel Michael as Captain of the Heavenly Hosts under a daisy in the head of the light and a scroll with 'St. Michael Archangel'. He is crowned, has large red wings, and he wears a white and blue halo, and armour. He holds a fiery sword and a pastoral staff, from which flies the banner of victory over death, with a red cross on a white ground. From it also hang the scales, symbolising equality and justice, in which a soul contemplating a crucifix in one pan weighs down the green dragon, representing the Devil and evil, which stands in the other. Underneath is a scroll with the text 'And the great dragon was cast out' (Revelation 12:9) and a picture of the fully armoured Archangel, who is wearing a coronet with a cross at the front and yellow wings and who is bearing a shield with a red cross as its device. His sword is raised over a grey winged Satan with horns, fangs and clawed hands, who is descending into yellow flames.

A Final Comment

It is sad that these windows have to be described as uninspiring. They confirm Martin Harrison's judgement that, after the First World War, much stained glass in England (and also in Wales), if it was not 'simply a debased version of either the Kempe-Comper or Arts and Crafts styles' was 'an example of the dismal decadence of one of the old-established

St. Paul's interior
(City and County of Swansea Library Service/G. Mills)

Victorian firms'. This assessment is the more galling because, in Swansea by the early 1950s, interesting stained glass was being produced whose aesthetic quality would have greatly enhanced St. Paul's by meeting more fully the criterion laid down by Henry Holiday that stained glass should 'adorn' the buildings in which it is erected.

In 1933, Howard Martin (1907-72) and his cousin, Hubert Thomas (1913-95), had set up a studio in Morriston. Two years later, Martin won one of the two scholarships which were awarded annually by the Worshipful Company of Glaziers and in 1939 a prescient commentator had remarked of his work that 'this stained glass work should one day win a reputation for Swansea'. In 1948, Martin and Thomas re-established themselves as Celtic Studios in Prospect Place, Swansea. By 1952, when Gerald Smith was first commissioned to design the windows for St. Paul's, the Studios had already begun to win important commissions in Swansea in churches such as St. Michael's, Manselton, St. David's, Morriston and All Saints, Oystermouth, with excellent designs which respected traditional ideas while working them with impeccable craftsmanship in a bold, and often exciting modern style. In St. Mary's, Swansea, which was re-consecrated in 1959, the stained glass was commissioned from James Powell & Co., which led one clergyman who attended the consecration to remark pointedly that he could see no justification for going to a London firm when so much excellent stained glass was being produced 'on our own door-step'. How unfortunate that St. Paul's too should have fallen foul of such a criticism.

A Note on the Fabrics

One decorative art which is often ignored is the fabrics of a church. It is particularly appropriate to describe them here since most of them have been designed and made by members of the congregation. They comprise vestments, altar frontals and pulpit falls and banners.

The vestments are four chasubles and stoles, all designed and made by Barbara Graham. The chasuble which is worn for celebrations of the Eucharist is made of cream damask on which there is a cross in silk appliqué and a central beaded decoration, based on the marble pattern in the sanctuary. For saints' days, the chasuble is of crimson silk with appliqué beads and embroidery. Its design in painted silk shows jagged, painful lines, overlaid with Pentecostal flames and beads, and with stitching designed to form fishes and the percussion instruments which were played by the young man to whom this vestment was posthumously dedicated. Two other chasubles are made of linen with log-cabin patchwork orphreys in silk; they are coloured green for use in Trinity and purple for Lent and Advent.

One High Altar frontal set has a central panel showing a shield charged with a Lamb and Flag and other motifs on either side, all in gold-work, which are believed to have come from the original frontal of 1850. There are traditional altar frontals manufactured by Vanpoulles in green for Trinity, purple for Lent and Advent and red for saints' days. A modern altar frontal was commissioned in memory of Derek Bule Williams, a churchwarden, and was designed and made by Iris Martin, who taught embroidery in the College of Art and at West Glamorgan Institute from 1945 to 1988. This frontal was badly damaged in a vestry fire in 1998, though the burse and veil, the superfrontal and the pulpit fall were all saved. The superfrontal has since been restored for future use.

The nave altar frontal and pulpit fall were made by Barbara Pyott following Iris Martin's original design. Three other frontals were designed by Viv Lewis, who also made the one for use in Lent, which shows a crown of thorns in wool on hessian. The Trinity frontal shows on a green ground a most attractive design of vine leaves and purple grapes, surrounded on four sides by five golden ears of barley, to represent the bread and wine of the Holy Communion; it was made by Betty Lamb. Jackie Rees designed and made the Advent frontal, using a design of a Celtic cross in yellow and gold-work against blue. The frontal for saints' days, displaying Pentecostal flames and the Dove of the Holy Spirit, was made by Barbara Graham and Margaret Jones.

The ten banners on the theme of the *Benedicite* – 'O all ye works of the Lord bless ye the Lord' – were designed variously by Barbara Price, Viv Lewis, Nyra Harris and Stella Rees and made by a group of church women.

In the Vivian chapel there are two processional banners. One, for the Mothers' Union made by Joy Luther Thomas, the wife of the vicar from 1969 to 1979, shows the Virgin Mary and Jesus, while the other one depicts St. Paul holding his attribute of a sword and a scroll with, below, the shields of the diocese and the Vivian family on either side of a shield with two crossed swords on a red ground. Another Mother's Union processional banner is in the sanctuary. It displays a lily, the symbol of purity and hence of the Virgin Mary, on light blue watered silk.

Finally, there is a credence cloth trimmed with bobbin lace by Margaret Jones, and, in the Vivian chapel, a set of offering-purses which were made out of the wedding-dress material which is believed to have been worn by Caroline Vivian in 1847.

Afterword

The millennium year has no religious significance apart from marking, rather inaccurately scholars now tell us, the two-thousandth year since the birth of Christ. It happened to coincide with the one hundred and fiftieth anniversary of the consecration of St. Paul's on 27th September 1850. It is a fitting time to take stock: to look back, as this book has, at what has been achieved, to review the present position of the church and parish and look to the future.

The parish has inherited a fine Victorian Gothic Revival church, designed by the distinguished architect, Henry Woodyer and classed by Elizabeth Beazley and Peter Howells in John Betjeman's *Collins Guide to the Parish Churches of England and Wales* as the 'finest in Swansea'. The church has, thanks to the vigilance of incumbents and church officers (not least that of Ken Lewis, its current Treasurer) and the generosity of parishioners, been cared for, repaired and enlarged over the years and is in good condition – an achievement all the more commendable when it is realised that the parish has the highest quota in the diocese (£48,982 in 2001).

St. Paul's has always had a high profile in the town and city. In Victorian times captains of industry, commercial magnates and distinguished lawyers occupied the offices of Vicar's Warden and People's Warden. Even in the less class-conscious past half-century it has had among its worshippers a large number who have made notable contributions to the community at large as well as to the church of which they were members. One thinks of Miss Isabel M. Westcott, a member of the English department at University College, Swansea who played an active role in the Student Christian Movement and in the social work conducted from the Old Strand Mission in Swansea. She wrote the play put on by the Dramatic Society for the 1950 anniversary celebrations and was responsible for the Great Pageant of the Prayer Book presented at the Swansea Guildhall for the Festival of Britain, 1951. Miss Edith Amy Smith, another regular worshipper, was the Matron of the Swansea General Hospital from 1941-1967. On her death in 2000 a memorial service was held for her at St. Paul's. Mr. Glyn Davies, formerly of Crown Printers, Morriston, a sidesman and P.C.C. secretary, played a major part in bringing the Ford Company to Swansea in the 1960s. Mr. John Barker, Royal Insurance Co., Swansea, inaugurated the Waste Paper Group in 1977. It had raised over £10,000 towards the upkeep of the church fabric before it was wound up in1989. He was a hard-working and enthusiastic Commissioner of Scouts in Swansea for a number of decades. Mr. Cyril Hughes, architect, served as a Diocesan Architect as well as Honorary Church Architect for St. Paul's. In the latter office he saved the church enormous sums of money by providing his services free of charge for the advice he gave and for the designs and plans he supplied for the church fabric and furnishings. Dr. Ellis Lloyd had served as a verger, but as Headmaster of Bishop Gore School (1950-65) forged a valuable link between the church and the school. Professor Roy and Mrs. Ena Knight worked hard for the establishment of All Souls church, the former writing the valuable history of that church for its jubilee in 1982. Both contributed much to the life and work of both St. Paul's and All Souls as well as to the College. Mr. Donald Coleman, a member of the choir, was M.P. for Neath from 1964 until his untimely death in 1991. He was referred to by the Revd. Garfield James in the parish magazine as 'our own Sketty church M.P.', when he took the choir over the House of Commons in 1978. Other public figures who worshipped at St. Paul's include Mr. D.V. Turner, Chief Constable of the Swansea Police Force between 1941 and 1962, who was a sidesman and member of the P.C.C. and did much good work for the Swansea Boys Club, and Superintendent Walter Hunt, author of *To Guard My People: An Account of the Origin and History of the Swansea Police.* More recently Mr. Henry Steane, churchwarden, was inaugurated as High Sheriff of West Glamorgan. The above list is of those known to the present writer. Parishioners who have known the church over a long period could doubtless add considerably to the list.

The parish has an enviable record for producing candidates for the priesthood. The following list is almost certainly incomplete but includes, with the years of their ordination to the priesthood: A.L.F. Norman (1932), K.J. Gillingham (1941), A.G. Howells (1957), D.B. James (1958), E.T. Hunt (1959), A.B. Evason (1960), R.L. Brown (1969), A.J. Knight (1976), A. Mort (1983), S.L. Wilson (1985), R. Hart (1986), and C.M.R. Jarvis (1999).

The parish has during the past half century had varying numbers of members serving on the Governing Body of the Church in Wales. As the year 2000 began six parishioners were serving on that body: Sue Knight (who is now training for the Ministry), Alan Hughes (since deceased), Elizabeth Rhodes, Carol Davies, Angela Ball and Nigel Doyle (who is now training for the non-stipendiary Ministry).

The half century from 1950 to 2000, has witnessed a marked decline in organised religion. Church statistics, which Bishop C.R. Sumner (d.1874), in a more expansive age, could refer to as 'the register of our moral power' now indicate how weak, quantitatively, that power has become, not only in Britain but in western Europe generally. Clifford Longley, writing in the *Daily Telegraph* (25.9.98) declared 'for the vast majority of those now under 35, religion has no effect on their lives whatever. However you measure it England is one of the most icily secular countries in the world – *perhaps only exceeded by Wales'* (my italics). Indeed the figures taken for the Church in Wales over a period are alarming. Vocations to the priesthood have fallen dramatically. Between 1850 and 1910 the number of ordained clergy in the four Welsh dioceses rose from 700 to 1,543 and was still around the 1,600 mark in the early 1930s. By 1959 the number had dropped to under 1,300 and by December 1999 the number had almost halved to 682 (stipendiary priests only). The Church in Wales has now fewer clergy than it had in 1850, before the great period of Victorian expansion in clerical manpower had begun.

The Church in Wales does not have a membership list as such, but such estimates as we have have been based on attendance parameters such as communicant numbers on feast days and a typical Sunday, the clergy's estimate of average Sunday attendance and on numbers on the electoral roll. A *Western Mail* survey in 1965 estimated that Church in Wales membership fell from 200,000 in 1953 to 180,000 in 1965. *Whitaker's Almanack, 2000* records the Church in Wales as having 'about 96,000 members', a figure which, even making allowances for the limitations of such estimates, may not be far from the true position. St. Paul's, Sketty has shared in this downward spiral of observance, as the following figures show:

	Baptisms	*Confirmations*	*Easter Communions*	*Electrol Roll*
1959	62	49	986	819
1999	26	9	387	488

For various reasons, among them the decline of the Sunday Schools and the failure of the sermon as an effective instrument of teaching, and the failure of both as a means of eliciting something more than temporary commitment, the Church has failed in the past century to pass on the Christian faith from generation to generation. It is all very well for people to say that a leaner church is a fitter church. If the present downward trend continues the organised church will just wither away.

But there are signs for hope, among them the Alpha courses, already adopted by St. Paul's. They now have such a proven track record as an effective instrument of mission that they should be advertised, encouraged and cultivated by every church. But something more is required. Darwinism, the bogey that had triggered the crisis of faith in the nineteenth century, has not gone away but has returned with a refined evolutionary theory, sometimes militantly expressed as an argument against Christian belief, and a new science of genetics, both posing crucial problems for theology and ethics. Science and religion are both legitimate windows on to reality. Clergy and people need to be able to engage intelligently with the new science. The Church needs, too, more media time for teaching and apologetics rather than for the sentimental, folksy fare that is sometimes transmitted. The wise and eloquent words which Bishop Glyn Simon delivered to the Governing Body in 1964 are as true today as when they were first delivered. He called for 'more holy bishops, more holy men and women', parishioners who would give so generously that the church could attempt 'vitalizing experiments and adventures, which keep us from stagnation, and which, even if they fail, preserve us from complacency, or an attitude of helplessly waiting upon events'.

These words should now be coupled with the words of our present Bishop Anthony in his address to the Diocesan Conference in 1999 on the urgent problems which confront the Church today and the need to develop a strategy for the future (*Diocesan News*, No. 93, 1999). He warns us of the dangers of focusing too much on heritage rather than on the Christian message:

> 'As far as the Christian faith is concerned the only reason for keeping a church, however beautiful or ancient, is that it continues to witness to a living faith. That it provides inspiration for the congregation to be a fine example of Christian care and compassion. That it really is an oasis of prayer and stillness where people can encounter the living God. That it is used as a base for mission in that reality. Our ancient churches were built to be signposts of the Gospel and not chapters in an architectural handbook. They are meant to be spiritual powerhouses and not historical theme parks.'

Lists of Incumbents, Assistant Clergy and Churchwardens

INCUMBENTS OF ST. PAUL'S, SKETTY

Edward A. Sanford	1850-1851
Montague Earle Welby	1851-1865
Edward William Bolney	1865-1903
Cecil George Campbell Lillingston	1903-1908
David Akrill-Jones	1909-1915
Henry John Stewart	1915-1941
Joseph Gwyn Davies	1941-1946
John Cyril Hill	1946-1950
Harry Craven Williams	1950-1958
Garfield Hughes James	1958-1979
Ilar Roy Luther Thomas	1979-1989
Stephen Brooks	1990-1993
Robert John Williams	1994-1999
Andrew James Knight	2000-

ASSISTANT CLERGY

D. Price	1897-1901
Lewis Davies	1901-1908
M.E. Davies	1905-1909
Gwilym Smith	1908-1910
Norman Parcell	1909-1924
Percy Rigby	1909-1911
Ll. P. Rees	1910-1914
Silas T. Phillips	1914-1915
D.D. Jones	1914-1919
R. Eustace Jones	1918-1921
David Lynne Davies	1921-1925
Edgar Osborne Williams	1923-1929
Vincent Gower Jones	1929-1932
Kenneth N.M. Earle	1932-1934
John James Absalom Thomas	1934-1936
George Rex Morgan	1936-1939
Henry Nicholas Hancock	1939-1945
Meredydd Howells	1945-1954
Ronald Henry Lloyd	1956-1959
Samuel Rhys Griffith	1957-1960
Dudley William White	1959-1966
Glyndwr Jones	1967-1970
John Alfred Morgan Jenkins	1962-1969
David Elwyn Rees	1969-1973
John Anthony Ellis	1972-1975
Robert Mar Erskine Paterson	1973-1978
Frank Kendall	1975-1978
Geoffrey Martin Reed	1978-1984
Jonathan Barker	1983-1984
Richard Hart	1985-1987
James Edwin Hansen	1987-1989
Peter William Hart	1989-1992
Rebecca Jane Dwyer	1991-1995
Graham Peter Noyce	1992-1994
Edward Michael Doyle	1994-1996
Susan Helen Jones	1995-1997
Jennifer Wigley	1998-
Martin Batchelor	1997-2000

Churchwardens

H. Hussey Vivian
John Crowe Richardson
W. Graham Vivian
John Coke Fowler
John Glasbrook
J. Clarke Richardson
Richard Glascodine
Felix Webber
J. Arthur Goode
H. Stanley Cook
Capt. W.H. Jenkins
S.A. Smith
John Chappell
James Isaac

Richard Monk
Stephen Morgan
S. Crocombe
Frank Thomas
A.T. Norman
A.F. Steele
J.E. Jones
E.M. Richards
James Jones
John Escott
J.E. Pratt
Cyril A. Hughes
W.H. Townsend
A.D. Frost

W.W. Hunt
E.P. Clement
D.B. Williams
Arthur H. Price
Graham Wattley
John A. Jones
Henry A. Steane
Carol Davies
Stuart J. Ball
Joyce Cole
James A. Davies
K. Clive Garrish

Glossary

AN EXPLANATION OF SOME OF THE SPECIAL TERMS USED AND INSTITUTIONS REFERRED TO IN THE TEXT

Some of the entries in the glossary are based on those in the following works:

ECEA – M.S. Briggs, *Everyman's Concise Encyclopaedia of Architecture* (London, 1959).

GTEA – T.D. Atkinson, *A Glossary of Terms used in English Architecture* (London, 7th ed. 1948).

ODCC – *Oxford Dictionary of the Christian Church*, ed. F.L. Cross, and E.A. Livingston (London, 3rd ed. 1997).

OED – *Compact Edition of the Oxford English Dictionary* (London, 2nd ed. 1993).

PDA – John Fleming and others, *The Penguin Dictionary of Architecture* (London, 4th ed. 1991).

Aesthetic Movement – A late C19 English and American artistic movement in reaction against 'Philistine' taste. It derived from the 'art for art's sake' theories of, among others, Walter Pater and Oscar Wilde. Its chief influence was on painting and the decorative arts and reached its apogee with the opening of the Grosvenor Gallery, London in 1877. PDA.

Ante-Communion – The first part of the Communion service down to the end of the prayer for the Church Militant in the Book of Common Prayer. Since the essential parts of the full rite (offering, consecration and communion) are omitted, it is not a real eucharist nor intended to be. It has parallels in the Mass of the Catechumens in the early church and in the Roman Catholic Dry Mass.

Arch-braced roof – A roof strengthened by pairs of curved braces forming an arch, usually connecting the wall or post below with the tie – or collar-beam above. PDA.

Arts and Crafts Movement – A late C19 English movement to revive handicrafts and reform architecture by using traditional building crafts and local materials. It was born in the wake of the 1851 Great Exhibition in London and in opposition to the machine-made furnishings made possible by the Industrial Revolution. It was inspired by John Ruskin and William Morris. PDA.

Aumbry – A cupboard either free standing or inserted in the wall of a church or sacristy where in medieval times books or sacred vessels were kept. It is now commonly used in churches of the Anglican communion as a secure place for the reserved sacrament.

Ballflower ornament – An enrichment carved in the hollow of a moulding consisting of a globular three-petalled flower enclosing a small ball. A decoration used in the late C13, throughout the C14 and in Gothic Revival buildings. PDA & GTEA.

Cadency-mark – In heraldry a variation in the same court of arms intended to show the descent of a younger branch from the main stock. OED.

Commoner – At Oxford University a student or undergraduate who pays for his commons. There were at one time many ranks of students: noblemen, commoners, battelers and servitors. Most are now obsolete and only scholars and commoners survive.

Crocket – A decorative spur of stone carved in various leaf shapes and projecting at regular intervals from the angles of spires, pinnacles, canopies and gables. PDA.

Cuddeston Theological College – A theological college near Oxford founded in 1854 by Bishop Samuel Wilberforce which became a centre of Tractarianism and high church influence.

Curvilinear tracery – A flowing style of tracery made up of compound or ogee curves, with an uninterrupted flow from curve to curve, also called undulating tracery. PDA.

Cusp – A point between the small arcs of trefoil and quatrefoil tracery.

Decorated style, also called Middle Pointed – A style of English Gothic architecture current between *c.*1250 and 1360 and revived in the C19. It is characterized by the use in window tracery of geometrical forms such as circles and quatrefoils and later of irregular shapes and flowing lines; the use of the ogee in the shaping of arches and window tracery and the enrichment of surfaces with at first stylized and later naturalistic foliage. The usual enrichments are the ball flower and the four leafed flower. The style was revived by the ecclesiologists of the nineteenth century and was considered by them as the best style for church building. Woodyer's use of the idiom in St. Paul's, Sketty, can be seen in the organ gallery over the sedilia, in the window tracery and in particular in the elaborately enriched hooded niches in the east wall of the Vivian chapel. GTEA.

Diaper work – All-over surface decoration of a small repeated pattern such as lozenges or squares. PDA.

Eastward position – This refers to (i) the turning of the clergy, choir and people to the east during the recitation of the Gospel and Creed and (ii) the position in the centre of the altar facing east adopted by the celebrant at the eucharist before the recent liturgical changes. See also North end.

English Church Union – A society founded in 1859 as 'The English Church Protection Society' and renamed 'The English Church Union' in 1860. It sought to defend and further the spread of high church principles in the Church of England, including the adoption of the 'Six Points': the eastward position, altar lights, eucharistic vestments, the mixed chalice, the use of unleavened bread in the eucharist and incense. It championed many priests during the ritual prosecutions. Charles Wood, later Viscount Halifax, exercised a powerful influence on the society after his election as its president in 1868. He was a close friend and Groom of the Bedchamber to Edward, Prince of Wales (later King Edward VII) who once remarked 'If ever I become religious, I should be of Charlie Wood's religion'.

Evangelical – 'An evangelical is one who believes in the supremacy of the Holy Spirit; within scripture, in conversion, in the life of the church and in the work of the ministry. Holiness of life, prayer, mission and evangelism, are integral to his personal life. And in the life of the Church, he desires Biblically based worship, sound and lively preaching, and a corporate identity'. (Roger Brown, *The Welsh Evangelicals*, p.2).

Exhibitioner – The holder of a scholarship or bursary in the form of a money grant given to a student from the funds of a school or college. OED.

Gothic Revival – An C18 and C19 movement to revive the Gothic style.

Keble College, Oxford – Founded in 1870 in memory of John Keble, one of the leaders of the Oxford Movement. It became a centre of Anglo-Catholic influence.

Knop – A decorated protuberance on the stem of a chalice to provide a grip for the celebrant at the eucharist.

Moderations – In Oxford University the first public examinations for the degree of B.A. conducted by the moderators.

Molet – In heraldry, a figure of a star, having five straight points . . . given as a mark for cadency for a third son. See cadency.

North end position – Throughout the greater part of the middle ages the celebrant at the eucharist stood facing east in a central position in front of a stone altar which was placed against or near the eastern wall of the church with the short ends on a north-south axis. In England and Wales during the Reformation changes of the C16 the stone altars were taken down and replaced with wooden tables. The rubric in the communion service of the Book of Common Prayer required the table to stand 'in the body of the church, or in the chancel . . . and the priest standing at the north side of the table . . .' In most churches the new communion table was placed in the chancel between the choir stalls 'tablewise', that is, with the short ends on an east-west axis with the celebrant in the centre of the north end facing south. The reformers argued that such a position avoided any notion of the priest offering a sacrifice or acting as a mediator between the people and God. After the restoration of church and monarchy in 1660 most churches were placing the communion table in its old position 'altarwise' against the east wall with the priest celebrating at the short north end facing south, thus obeying the rubric. Even leaders of the Oxford movement such as Pusey and Newman celebrated in this way. The eastern position was declared illegal by the Purchas Judgement of 1871 (see Purchas Judgement). The judgement soon became a dead letter and new generations of churchmen gradually adopted the eastward position until the liturgical changes of the 1960s recommended the moving of the altar so that the priest could celebrate facing the people.

Ogee – A double-curved line made up of a convex and concave part; the term is especially applied to arches and mouldings. GTEA

Oxford Movement – A religious movement within the Church of England started in 1833 by clerical members of the University of Oxford, especially J.H. Newman, John Keble and E.B. Pusey. Initially a movement directed against theological liberalism and the interference of the state in church affairs, it sought to restore the high church principles of the C17 and to emphasise the Catholic doctrine implicit in the rubrics and text of the Book of Common Prayer. The principles of the movement were promulgated through a series of *Tracts for the Times* (see *Tractarianism*). It had a decisive effect in raising standards of worship in the Church of England. Many of the followers of the movement began calling themselves Anglo-Catholics and urged the revival of ritual and ceremonial and the use of vestments which they claimed was ordered by the ornaments rubric of the 1662 Book of Common Prayer. ODCC.

Pensioner – At Cambridge University, an undergraduate who is not a scholar or a sizar; one who pays for his own commons or expenses. Equivalent to a commoner at Oxford.

Perpetual curate – Where the rectory of a parish has been appropriated and there has been no endowment of a vicarage, the benefice is a perpetual curacy. The appropriator or patron is bound to nominate the curate to serve the parish, and has no power to remove him after he has been licensed by the bishop, and hence the name 'perpetual'. J.S. Purvis, *Dictionary of Ecclesiastical Terms* (London, 1962), p.145.

Purchas Judgement – The judgement by the Judicial Committee of the Privy Council in 1871 against the Revd. John Purchas, vicar of St. James, Brighton, which declared that eucharistic vestments, the eastward position, the mixed chalice and the use of unleavened bread were illegal, reversing a previous decision by the Dean of Arches. ODCC.

Puseyite – A churchman committed to the principles of the Tractarian or Oxford Movement. The term was derived from one of its leaders, E.B. Pusey, who was probably singled out because he was the first contributor to the *Tracts for the Times* to append his initials to a tract (No. 18, 1833). ODCC.

Quarry – A square or diamond shaped pane of glass with which medieval style leaded windows are glazed or any small quadrangular opening in the tracery of a window. PDA.

Rectilinear – A style of tracery in which vertical and horizontal lines predominate in its design. Associated with the Perpendicular style of architecture in England *c.*1360-*c.*1550. ECEA.

St. David's College, Lampeter – The oldest Welsh degree granting institution. Founded in 1822 by Bishop Thomas Burgess of St. David's for Church of England students, it became a constituent college of the University of Wales in 1971. Bishop Burgess Theological Hall at Lampeter closed in 1976.

Scissor-braced roof – A roof strengthened by pairs of braces which cross diagonally between pairs of rafters or principals. PDA.

Sedilia – inset seats for the clergy in the sanctuary.

Tractarianism – A name for the early stages of the Oxford Movement derived from the *Tracts for the Times* which were aimed at disseminating Church principles 'against Popery and Dissent'. The first, penned by J.H. Newman in 1833, dealt with the doctrine of the Apostolic Succession. The last, Tract 90

(1841) was on the Thirty-Nine Articles and was also by Newman. John Aubrey Vivian's copies of the Tracts, in bound volumes, are held by the Library of University of Wales, Swansea (see also Oxford Movement).

Trefoil – The lobes or leaf-shaped curves formed by the cusping of a circle or an arch are called foils and the number involved are indicated by the prefix, e.g. trefoil, quatrefoil. PDA.

Wycliffe Hall, Oxford – A theological college founded in 1877 by evangelicals which became a centre of evangelical influence.

Bibliography

MANUSCRIPTS AND RECORDS

ABERYSTWYTH. National Library of Wales. Department of Manuscripts.
Church in Wales records. Visitation returns.
Vivian papers.
LONDON. Lambeth Palace Library.
Incorporated Church Building Society files Nos. 10749, 11857.
SWANSEA. West Glamorgan Archive Service.
St. Paul's Church, Sketty Records.
SWANSEA. Central Reference Library
Items referring to Sketty and St. Paul's church in the cuttings file.
Odd numbers of parish magazines and reports.

PRINTED WORKS

BARKER, T.W. *Particulars relating to the endowments etc. of livings. Vol. I: Archdeaconry of Carmarthen* (Carmarthen, 1907).

BROADY, M. 'An undervalued Welsh art: Celtic Studios' stained glass 1933-1992', *Minerva*, IV (1996), 3-16.

BROADY, M. 'A vision fulfilled: the start of the Welsh stained glass tradition', *The Journal of Stained Glass*, XIX (1991-3), 197-215.

BROADY, M. 'Departed glory: Celtic Studios: The firm and its glass 1948-1992', *The Journal of Stained Glass*, XXI (1997), 44-67.

BROWN, R.L. 'A new vicarage for Sketty', *Minerva*, V (1998), 15-20.

BROWN, R.L. 'A well-heeled gadfly: Montague Earle Welby' (unpublished paper).

BROWN, R.L. *The Welsh evangelicals* (Cardiff, 1986).

BURTON, Ian (Archimandrite Barnabas) *Strange pilgrimage* (Welshpool, 1985).

CHURCH IN WALES. *The constitution of the Church in Wales* (Cardiff, Rev. ed. 1964).

CHURCH IN WALES. *Directory/yearbook/official hand book* (Cardiff, 1925, 1930, 1936, 1939, 1957).

CLARK, K. *The Gothic revival* (London, 1928, repr. 1995)

COWLEY, F.G. 'Religion and education' in *Swansea: an illustrated history*, ed. Glanmor Williams (Swansea, 1990).

CROCKFORD'S CLERICAL DIRECTORY. Various years.

DAVIES, P. & MORGAN, D. *1926-76: Parish of Killay, St. Hilary's Church, Jubilee Brochure* (Killay, 1976).

DIOCESE OF SWANSEA AND BRECON. *Diocesan handbook/yearbook and directory*. Various years.

EMMERSON, R. *Church plate* (London, 1991).
EVANS, G. *Dunvant: portrait of a community.* (Stafford, 1992).
EVANS, J.T. *The church plate of Gowerland.* (Stow-on-the-Wold,1921).
FOSTER, J. *Alumni Oxonienses: the members of the University of Oxford, 1715-1886* (Oxford, 4 vols, 1888).
FOWLER, W.W. *A brief memoir of John Coke Fowler, late stipendiary magistrate of Swansea, and formerly chairman of Quarter Sessions for the County of Glamorgan* (Oxford,1901).
FOWLER, J.C. *Church pews, their origin and legal incidents: with some observations on the propriety of abolishing them.* (London, 1844).
GILBERT, A.D. *Religion and society in industrial England.* (London, 1976).
GIROUARD, M. *Sweetness and light: the Queen Anne movement 1860-1900.* (London, 1977).
GRICE, F. *Who's who in Kilvert's diary* (Hereford, 1977).
GRIFFITHS, R.A. *Clyne Castle, Swansea: a history of the building and its owners.* (Swansea, 1977).
GRIFFITHS, R.A. *Singleton Abbey and the Vivians of Swansea.* (Landysul, 1988).
HARRISON, M. *Victorian stained glass.* (London, 1980).
HARRISON, M. & WATERS, B. *Burne-Jones.* (London, 1990).
HASTINGS, A. *A history of English Christianity, 1920-1985.* (London,1986).
HOLIDAY, H. *Stained glass as an art.* (London, 1896).
HOWELLS, R. *A tale of two grandmothers: memoirs of an ecumenist, 1965-85.* (Swansea, 1994).
JONES, S. 'The Vivian family', *Port Talbot Historical Society Trans.* II. (1974), 5-17.
KILVERT, F. *Selections from the diary of the Revd. Francis Kilvert 23 August 1871-13 May 1874.* Edited by William Plomer. 3 volumes. (London, Rev. ed. 1960).
KNIGHT, R. *Silver jubilee: the Church of All Souls, Tycoch, 1957-1982.* (Tycoch, 1982).
LEWIS, J. *The Swansea guide.* (Swansea, 1851, repr. 1989).
LUCAS, R.L.T. 'The false signals of Rhosilly', *Gower,* XXIX (1978), 31-37.
MORRIS, B. *The houses of Singleton: a Swansea landscape.* (Swansea, 1995).
NEALE, J.M. *Church enlargement and church arrangement.* (Cambridge, 1843).
NEALE, J.M. 'S. David, Sketely [sic], Gower, in Glamorganshire', *The Ecclesiologist,* XI (1850), 145.
NEWMAN, J. *Glamorgan* (Buildings of Wales series) (London, 1995).
ORRIN, G.R.& COWLEY, F.G. *A history of All Saints Church, Oystermouth.* (Llandysul, 1990).
OXFORD DICTIONARY OF THE CHRISTIAN CHURCH, ed. E.A. Livingstone (Oxford, 3rd ed. 1997).
PAINTING, D. *Amy Dillwyn.* (Cardiff, 1987).
PRICE, D.T.W. 'The Revd. Montague Earle Welby', *Kilvert Society Newsletter,* 1990 (2), pp. 3-6.
PRICE, D.T.W. *A history of the Church in Wales in the twentieth century.* (Cardiff, 1990).

PUGSLEY, J. *Reminiscences of definite church progress in Swansea & neighbourhood during the last twenty years.* (Swansea,1906).

PUGSLEY, J. *Church life and thought in Swansea and neighbourhood . . . Progress of the Oxford Movement locally. Past and present reminiscences.* (Swansea, 1915).

REED, J.S. *Glorious battle: the cultural politics of Victorian Anglo-Catholicism* (Nashville, 1996).

REYNOLDS, P. *Saint Gabriel's: a centenary history of the parish of St. Gabriel with Saint Augustine, Swansea, 1889-1989.* (Swansea, 1989).

St. Paul's, Langleybury: the first hundred years. (Langleybury, 1964).

St. Paul's, Sketty: a souvenir, 1910. (Swansea, 1910 Repr. 1999).

SMITH, J.A. *The Welsh Church: What is she doing? A sermon preached at Sketty Church on Sunday morning June 5th 1887 on the occasion of the visit of the Right Hon. W.E. Gladstone M.P. to Swansea.* (Cardiff, 1887).

SOWERS, R. *Stained glass: an architectural art.* (London, 1965).

STAVVIDI, M. *Master of glass: Charles Eamer Kempe, 1837-1907.* (Hatfield, 1988).

STEWART, A. *Family tapestry.* (London, 1961).

THIRWALL, C. *A sermon by Connop Thirlwall, D.D., bishop of St. David's delivered at the consecration of St. Paul's, Sketty on Friday, September 27th, 1850.* (Swansea, 1850).

THOMAS, N.L. *The story of Swansea's districts and villages.* (Swansea, 2nd ed. 1969).

TOOMEY, R.R. *Vivian and Sons, 1809-1924: a study of the firm in the copper and related industries.* (New York, 1985).

TREW, W.H. *Christ Church, Swansea, 1872-1972: centenary brochure.* (Swansea, 1972).

VENN, J.A. *Alumni Cantabrigienses: a biographical list of all known students . . . 1752-1900.* (Cambridge, 6 vols., 1940-54).

VIVIAN, H.H. *Disestablishment and disendowment from a churchman's point of view. A speech delivered on 25th November 1885.* (Swansea, 1885).

WALKER, D. *A short history of the parish church of Swansea.* (Swansea, 3rd rev. ed., 1967).

WALKER, D. *The first hundred years: St. James church, Swansea, 1867-1967.* (Swansea, 1967).

WALKER, D. *Nerth yr eglwys.* (Morriston, 1964). (English text).

WALKER, D. and M. *Swansea and Brecon, 1923-1973: a jubilee of the diocese.* (Swansea, 1973).

WALKER, M.S. *Beguildy to Rhosili: the story of the growth of the Mothers' Union within the diocese of Swansea and Brecon.* (Cardiff, 1989).

WILLIAMS, E.G. *'Move on!' or, church progress in Swansea and suburbs during the last fifty years.* (Swansea, 1889).

WILLIAMS, H.C. *The story of St. Paul's church, Sketty 1850-1950.* (Morriston, 1950).

Index